T0338407

ORGANIZING
IN HARD TIMES

In the Series
Labor and Social Change,
edited by Paula Rayman and Carmen Sirianni

LOUISE B. SIMMONS

ORGANIZING IN HARD TIMES

Labor and Neighborhoods in Hartford

TEMPLE UNIVERSITY PRESS

PHILADELPHIA

Temple University Press, Philadelphia 19122
Copyright © 1994 by Temple University. All rights reserved
Published 1994
Printed in the United States of America

Library of Congress Cataloging-in-Publication Data

Simmons, Louise B., 1949-
    Organizing in hard times : labor and neighborhoods in Hartford /
Louise B. Simmons.
        p.   cm.—(Labor and social change)
    Includes bibliographical references and index.
    ISBN 1-56639-155-5.—ISBN 1-56639-156-3 (pbk.)
    1. Trade-unions—Connecticut—Hartford—Organizing.
    2. Unemployment—Connecticut—Hartford.   3. Neighborhood—
Connecticut—Hartford.   I. Title.   II. Series.
HD6490.072U68   1994
331.88'09746'3—dc20   93-33184

For my family,
my friends,
and my struggling community of Hartford

CONTENTS

A C K N O W L E D G M E N T S

There are so many people who were important in this effort. First, I would like to acknowledge my family—my parents, Louis and Frances Simmons, my sister, Wendy Simmons, who pursued her doctorate simultaneously with me, my partner, Peter Chenette, and his daughter, Emily, for their love and support throughout the process of writing the dissertation on which this book is based, and then the book itself. I am very indebted to Temple University Press, particularly its editor-in-chief, Michael Ames, and series editor Paula Rayman for their review and assistance in finalizing this book. My dissertation committee at MIT, Gary Marx, Phillip Clay, and Michael Lipsky, were very constructive and challenging in their comments, suggestions, and guidance. Many of my colleagues at the University of Connecticut School of Social Work, as well as my students, were also very supportive. Anthony Maluccio, now of Boston College, was extremely encouraging and helped me get started. Several friends and colleagues reviewed drafts of this book, and I am grateful for their ideas: James Miller, Kenneth Neubeck, and Sue Tenorio.

Hartford as a social environment provided poignant examples of social movements from which to select examples to analyze. I thank the entire community of activists and the participants in all of the movements and organizations. Especially to the six organizations, the several coalitions, and all of their respective participants highlighted in the book I owe incredible gratitude. Their willingness to allow me access and provide me with all types of information made this entire project possible.

Although it is not possible to list every person, the following individuals in numerous ways provided information and support and encouragement to continue the commuting, researching, writing, and thinking: in Boston, from the Department of Urban Studies and Planning at MIT, Louise Dunlap and Bennett Harrison, now of Carnegie Mellon; the presence and kindness offered by Mel King was also a great inspiration. Two individuals in Boston were particular sources of strength to me, Françoise Carré and Polly Halfkenny.

In Hartford, the following friends and activists were the backbone of the effort: from 1199—Jerry Brown, Merrilee Milstein, Pearl Granat (who was extremely helpful in reviewing the section on the Blitz model), Kevin Doyle, Carmen Boudier, Bill Myerson, David Pickus, former officer John Fussell, and all of the other officers, staff, and members; from the UAW—John Flynn, Phil Wheeler, Bob Madore, Charlene Block, Russ See, and other Region 9A and Local 376 officers, staff, and members, but particularly all of the Colt strikers, whose courage and dedication were among the most remarkable things the Hartford area has witnessed in many years; from Local 217—Connie Holt, former Secretary-Treasurer Henry Tamerin, former organizer Rob Traber, all the Hartford area members and former members, and in particular the former Sheraton strikers; from HART—former and current directors Nancy Ardema and Jim Boucher and the organizers and many activists; from AHOP—former directors Mike Gorzach and Kevin Kelly, former organizers George Jefferson and Lourdes Colon, and other staff and activists, particularly the tenants in the formerly Early-owned buildings; from ONE-CHANE—former director Patricia Wrice and former organizer Tom Connolly (who as a social work colleague kindly reviewed my material on neighborhood organizing); all of the People for Change activists, especially Bill Hagan, Mary McAtee, Steve Thornton, John Murphy, Denise Viera, John Bonelli, Sandra Little, and other Steering Committee members and activists; Labor Council president Kip Lockhart; all of the participants in the Community-Labor Alliance, but especially Rochelle Ripley and Laddie Michalowski; UCAN consultant Alta Lash; Rick Kozin; Richard Ratcliff; Bernard Magubane; Howard Stanback;

two special South African friends, Kumi Naidoo and Dan Pillay; Brian Steinberg, Mina Mina, Susan Gluck, Elizabeth Horton Sheff, Nicholas Fusco, and countless other friends and colleagues. I continue to draw inspiration from the leadership of former Hartford mayor Carrie Saxon Perry, whose personal support is deeply appreciated.

ORGANIZING
IN HARD TIMES

City Neighborhoods, City of Hartford,
with Neighborhood Organization Boundaries
Source: City of Hartford Planning Department

Introduction

Hartford, Connecticut, is a dramatic and compact example of contemporary urban dilemmas in the United States. In their neighborhoods and their workplaces, Hartford's people feel the impact of economic change. They observe the booms and busts of downtown development, the rise and fall of real estate empires, shifting employment opportunities as firms in all sectors retrench, and varying levels of interest or concern from both private and public policymakers. Their public services erode as ever more complex demands on these services arise. Life in Hartford is full of both hope and grave problems: hope that opportunity can still be created in urban America and the reality of simmering problems too long ignored or brushed aside.

During the 1980s, Hartford gained the unfortunate distinction of being the fourth-poorest city in the country, using the measure of percentage of population in poverty: Within its 17.2 square miles, 25.2 percent of the 136,000 people lived below the poverty level. In the 1990 census, a similar analysis revealed that while poverty in Hartford grew to 27.5 percent of its 139,000 people, it had become the eighth-poorest city in the country, behind such additions to the ten poorest cities as Laredo (Texas), Detroit, Flint, Cleveland, and Gary (Lipton 1992).

While it is the capital city of the state with the consistently highest per capita income in the country ($21,226 in 1987, for example), Hartford is Connecticut's poorest city, with a 1987 per capita income of $8,677. Hartford also has the nation's second-highest child poverty rate: Over 39 percent of its children live in poverty, many in single-parent households headed by women (McCarthy 1988). Infant mortality rates resemble those of impoverished third-world nations, owing in large part to inadequate prenatal care and high levels of teenage pregnancy. Shortages of affordable housing, soaring crime rates, youth gangs, drug trafficking, a tragically high incidence of AIDS, racial segregation and isolation within the city's educational system, and a litany of other compelling problems contribute to a truly distressed social environment.

This pervasive poverty is ringed by affluent suburbs with a very different social structure. While Hartford's population in 1990 was 36 percent African American and 32 percent Hispanic, the neighboring thirty-seven towns in the Hartford PMSA (primary metropolitan statistical area) were over 92 percent white. Put another way, while Hartford houses only 18 percent of the 768,000 people who live in the metropolitan area, 65 percent of the area's Black population and 76 percent of its Hispanic population live in the city of Hartford (Hartford Planning Department 1991). White households in the region enjoyed an average income of $24,749 in 1980, while Black household incomes averaged $15,812, and Hispanic $12,694 (Williams 1988). By 1990 over 92 percent of the 27,000 public school students in Hartford were Black, Hispanic, or of other minorities, and a landmark school desegregation suit, *Sheff v. O'Neill,* was filed to address this imbalance.

As stark as the differences between Hartford and its suburbs are, the contrast between Hartford's downtown and its neighborhoods is perhaps even more striking. Local actors describe Hartford as a "tale of two cities" within one geopolitical boundary. Downtown Hartford exploded with development during the 1980s. Gleaming modern skyscrapers, congested streets, fancy boutiques, and a civic center that hosts home games of the city's National Hockey League franchise, the Whalers, transformed the small, rather sleepy, commercial district of twenty years ago into a truly thriving regional financial center.

Hartford's downtown skyline in the late 1980s was dramatically different from even ten years earlier. New development in Hartford's downtown took place quite rapidly. In the first half of the 1980s, downtown office space more than doubled: Between 1980 and mid-1986 over 5 million new square feet of downtown office space was built (Hartford Planning Department, June 1986). By mid-1988, a total of 9.29 million square feet of office space existed in downtown Hartford, and 1.1 million was under construction (Pazniokas 1988). When development abruptly ceased in the late 1980s, many proposed projects fell victim to the recession credit crunch and the lack of demand for office space. While Hartford boasted the tightest market for downtown office space in the country through 1988 (with vacancy rates as low as 5 to 7 percent; Horgan 1988), by early 1989 vacancy rates for Class A space rose to over 10 percent and continued to rise to over 12 percent in the early nineties.

The corporate headquarters of several major national insurance companies, preeminent among them Travelers Insurance and Aetna Life and Casualty, as well as the headquarters of defense giant United Technologies, are located in downtown Hartford. The insurance companies' presence in particular provides the drive, and often the financing, for local development. Yet, by the end of the 1980s, the economic crash of the northeastern real estate market had taken its toll on Hartford: Several large vacant spaces, sites of demolished buildings that had been leveled to make way for new skyscrapers, pockmarked the compact downtown business district.

EMPLOYMENT AND THE ECONOMIC AND CORPORATE BASE

Employment trends in Hartford are a key indicator of economic change in the city. In 1960 manufacturing accounted for 21 percent (approximately 24,300 jobs) of the city's nonagricultural employment. By 1990, over 17,000 manufacturing jobs had left the city, and manufacturing accounted for only 4.4 percent of the employment within the city. Despite the loss within the city of Hartford, manufacturing jobs increased in the larger Hartford labor market area (LMA) after 1960, peaking at 100,400 in 1980. By 1990, however, the number of manufacturing jobs had dropped to 83,400.

Even before the 1980s, employment in the city of Hartford was concentrated more and more in the financial/insurance/real estate (FIRE) and service sectors (see Table 1). Throughout the period 1960–1985 Hartford was also losing its share of the total employment in the labor market area; it dropped from 41.2 percent in 1970 to 34.9 percent in 1983 (Hartford Commission on the City Plan 1984). Moreover, Hartford residents' participation in the labor force was lower in 1980 than in 1960, though the total number of jobs in Hartford increased significantly in that time (see Table 2).

Most of the jobs created in Hartford during the 1980s were in the service sector. Job creation peaked in 1988 and then began to decline as the economy slid into the recession. Manufacturing steadily declined, the government sector increased, FIRE fluctuated, and the level of service sector employment climbed both relatively and absolutely (see Table 3).

Job creation within the Hartford LMA during the 1980s occurred largely within the service sector, though gains were also made in the FIRE and government sectors (see Table 4).

Unemployment in both the city of Hartford and the Hartford LMA rose precipitously as the recession took hold: In 1988 Hartford experienced a 5.8 percent unemployment rate; in 1989, 6.8 percent; and in 1990, 8.7 percent. For the LMA, the rates were 2.8 percent, 3.3 percent, and 4.5 percent, respectively (Connecticut Department of Labor 1990a, 1991a, 1991b).

Although manufacturing was not a significant part of the city of Hartford's economic base by the late 1980s, it was still significant, but declining, in the larger labor market area. The largest manufacturing concern in the area, the Pratt and Whitney Division of United Technologies located in neighboring East Hartford, employed some eight thousand to ten thousand people throughout this period and supported a supplier network that included many local companies.

T A B L E I

Nonagricultural Employment in the City of Hartford: Selected Sectors, 1965–1980

EMPLOYMENT SECTOR	1965		1970		1975		1980	
Total jobs	117,780	100.2%	134,450	100.1%	125,450	99.0%	143,180	100.0%
Manufacturing	23,100	19.6%	20,030	14.9%	11,600	9.2%	12,210	8.5%
FIRE[a]	28,450	24.4%	35,040	26.1%	38,020	30.3%	45,200	31.6%
Service	21,900	18.6%	25,690	19.1%	29,023	23.1%	34,560	24.1%
Government	12,980	11.0%	20,530	15.3%	20,870	16.6%	22,720	15.9%
Other[b]	31,350	26.6%	33,160	24.7%	24,937	19.8%	28,490	19.9%

Source: Connecticut Department of Labor.

Note: Percentages may not total exactly 100 because of rounding.

[a]Financial/insurance/real estate.

[b]"Other" includes employment in construction, transportation, communications and utilities, and trade.

T A B L E 2

Hartford Residents' Participation in the Labor Force, 1960–1980

	1960	1970	1980	CHANGE 1960–1980
Jobs in Hartford	115,840	134,450	143,180	+27,340
Hartford labor force	77,855	71,408	61,688	−16,167

Source: Connecticut Department of Labor and U.S. Census, as compiled in *Hartford: State of the City* (September 1983).

However, in early 1992, United Technologies announced a massive restructuring program and work-force reductions of immense proportions, involving the eventual loss of over five thousand jobs in its Connecticut operation and the closing of its Southington plant.

Hartford was once home to many large factories, such as Fuller Brush, Royal Typewriter, Underwood Typewriter, and others that employed thousands of workers. Well before the beginning of the 1980s, many of these businesses had closed, moving their operations either to the southern part of the United States or overseas, or simply closing up shop. Royal Typewriter Company employed several thousand people before moving its operations to England in 1972. The Underwood Typewriter plant in Hartford closed even earlier, in 1968, throwing close to two thousand workers out of their jobs. Underwood was purchased by the Italian concern Olivetti and became known as Olivetti-Underwood. After several years of maintaining the Hartford plant, the company decided to consolidate its operations and closed the local plant. The Underwood plant was demolished and new office and residential development took place on the property, but the Royal factory lay vacant and undeveloped until 1992, when most of it was destroyed by a fire.

The growth in the insurance sector over the past several decades coincides with the diversification of the insurance industry, which is now involved in a vast array of financial activities from real estate

TABLE 3

Nonagricultural Employment in the City of Hartford: Selected Sectors, 1980–1990

EMPLOYMENT SECTOR	1980		1982		1984		1986		1988		1990	
Total jobs	143,180	100.0%	137,220	99.9%	142,890	100.0%	152,650	100.1%	158,600	99.9%	151,380	100.0%
Manufacturing	12,210	8.5%	11,020	8.0%	9,390	6.6%	9,720	6.4%	8,260	5.2%	6,620	4.4%[c]
FIRE[a]	45,200	31.6%	43,760	31.9%	45,550	31.9%	46,690	30.6%	46,050	29.0%	43,020	28.4%
Service	34,560	24.1%	35,870	26.1%	39,630	27.7%	43,950	28.8%	50,190	31.6%	48,540	32.1%
Government	22,720	15.9%	20,200	14.7%	20,980	14.7%	23,010	15.1%	24,340	15.3%	24,890	16.4%[d]
Other[b]	28,490	19.9%	26,370	19.2%	27,340	19.1%	29,280	19.2%	29,760	18.8%	28,310	18.7%

Source: Connecticut Department of Labor.

Note: Percentages may not total exactly 100 because of rounding.

[a]Financial/insurance/real estate.

[b]"Other" includes employment in construction, transportation, communications and utilities, and trade.

[c]In 1990 the Colt strikers returned to work.

[d]Government sector employment peaked in 1989 at 25,410 and then declined in 1990.

T A B L E 4

Job Creation in the Hartford Labor Market Area:
Selected Sectors, 1980–1990

EMPLOYMENT SECTOR	1980	1990	CHANGE 1980–1990
Total jobs	396,200	477,700	(net)+81,500
Manufacturing	100,400	83,400	−17,000
FIRE	60,300	75,000	+14,700
Service	74,600	116,300	+41,700
Government	53,800	63,600	+9,800
Other[a]	107,100	139,400	

Source: Connecticut Department of Labor.
[a]"Other" includes employment in construction, transportation, communications and utilities, and trade.

development to pension fund management and other financial services. These companies have deep historical roots in Hartford. Several have been in the city since colonial times, when merchants involved in insurance underwriting formed Connecticut's first insurance company in 1810, the Hartford Fire Insurance Company— today a subsidiary of ITT. The Aetna Insurance Company was founded in 1819. Other companies were formed in the 1850s and 1860s, including Travelers in 1864 ("A City Built on Risk" 1986).

Throughout the twentieth century the insurance companies have undertaken large construction projects with far-reaching impact on Hartford's physical and economic growth. Earlier in the century their own expanding work forces and office space requirements drove the construction of office buildings as well as the development of housing for their employees. In recent decades they have played a role in all phases of Hartford's development: Aetna financed the construction of the Hartford Civic Center. Aetna and ITT, the parent company of the Hartford Insurance Group, financed the adjoining Sheraton Hotel. Yet the insurance companies themselves are undergoing substantial restructuring in an attempt to become leaner. Between 1988 and 1989, Travelers eliminated 1,100 jobs in an attempt to cut its costs by 40 percent ("More Job Loss at Travelers" 1989). In 1992, 500 Connecticut jobs were eliminated in a "strategic alliance" leading to an eventual merger with Primerica Corporation. Aetna and other firms have likewise downsized.

An unusual chapter in corporate-community relations described both by Neubeck and Ratcliff (1988) and Clavel (1986) is the history of the "Hartford Process," a corporate-sponsored think tank supported by the insurance companies and major banking concerns. It existed during the 1970s under several different organizational incarnations as a private sector planning organization and undertook several controversial projects.

Neubeck and Ratcliff (1988) recount the history of Hartford Process's plans for a Rouse-inspired new community in rural eastern Connecticut that would house the Hartford residents to be displaced by new development in the central city. None of these plans was acted upon by city planning bodies, the city council, or any municipal authority. When reaction to the plan both in the rural community, which would be the site of the new development, and in Hartford's North End was overwhelmingly unfavorable, the scheme was abandoned and Hartford Process set its sights on less grandiose projects.

At one point a "confidential memo" from a Process staff member to its board of directors was leaked to the public, and another huge outcry occurred. The memo detailed a set of plans for downtown development "predicated on a geo-political strategy" that included gentrification, a managed population mix of racial and ethnic groups, curtailment of Puerto Rican migration to Hartford, and the marshaling of resources to protect remaining middle-class neighborhoods in Hartford. The city's Puerto Rican community was particularly offended by the memo and held a demonstration that formed a human chain around the civic center during its first months of operation.

Hartford Process is one example of elite behavior in Hartford. Neubeck and Ratcliff (1988) chronicle many other examples of activity by the insurance companies and major banks to maintain their dominance in the development arena and point out that the ability of the neighborhood forces to influence such events varies. They argue that neighborhood forces can at best check only the most offensive aspects of development but cannot harness the requisite power to have a substantial impact on the course of development. Only minimal concessions are occasionally granted to community organizations, and when the battle lines are really drawn, as in the struggle by community forces to enact a development tax known as "linkage," the corporations have the ability to "circle the wagons" and hold out for their position. Neubeck and Ratcliff offer little hope that the neighborhood organizations will be able to counter the adverse effects of recent development trends in the cities.

RESPONSES AND ACTIVISM

While fortunes were made during the 1980s, only to be lost as the nineties unfolded, many people in Hartford did not enjoy any newfound wealth or buying power, especially the city's poor and working-class populations. In their workplaces and neighborhoods they found ways to express their frustration. Consider one week in March 1988.

On March 11, tenants affiliated with the Asylum Hill Organizing Project marched into the office of Hartford city manager Alfred Gatta with bags of garbage. They had collected the garbage from a building owned by a notorious slumlord who had recently been given an extension by city officials on court-mandated improvements. Two days earlier, members of the New England Health Care Employees–District 1199 took over the office of Anthony Milano, director of the State of Connecticut Office of Policy and Management, demanding state action on the nursing shortage in state of Connecticut health care institutions. Throughout the same week, on the twenty-first floor of a recently constructed skyscraper in down-town Hartford, in the National Labor Relations Board's Hartford office, an administrative law judge concluded daily sessions in a lengthy trial over a two-year-old continuing strike by the United Auto Workers against Colt Firearms. Meanwhile, an emerging political organization—People for Change—fresh from stunning successes in local elections, was about to begin a one-and-one-half day conference to chart its future. This one week of activity is a good example of how the people of Hartford, by some very innovative and diverse means, are fashioning responses to the economic changes transpiring in their city. Living in Hartford, as I have for over twenty years, one cannot avoid being affected by these movements and issues. But being involved in them, as I have also been, offers a wealth of material about how people adapt to economic change.

Political Developments

Hartford's recent political history reflects the growing political organization of the city's African American and Puerto Rican communities as well as the increasing needs and claims of the population on a fragmented city government. The structure of municipal government is an odd mixture of reform and tradition. Since charter revisions in the 1940s and 1960s, the local govern-ment consists of a nine-member city council elected at large, with three seats reserved (per state statute) for a minority party; a city manager, who serves as the city's chief administrative officer and who is selected (and can be dismissed) by the city council; and an elected mayor, whose position is visible but lacking in authority. Numerous commissions and authorities exert their own power and influence, such as the Redevelopment Authority and the Zoning Board of Appeals. A referendum to revise the city charter, granting more power to the mayor's office and establishing a mixed-district/at-large council, was unsuccessful in 1993.

The city is solidly Democratic: Registered Democrats outnumber registered Republicans by more than seven to one. Hartford went for George McGovern in 1972, Jimmy Carter in 1976 and 1980, Walter Mondale in 1984, Michael Dukakis in 1988, and Bill Clinton in 1992. Jesse Jackson won resounding primary victories in Hartford in both 1984 and 1988. Given this intense loyalty to the Democratic party within the city's population, intraparty divisions and contests are what fuel the political fires of Hartford. The factions of the Democratic party in Hartford, like those in New York City (Katznelson 1981), tend to organize around race, ethnicity, and territoriality. These bases of organization, in turn, reflect the city's segregated housing patterns.

In describing modern American urban politics, Katznelson (1981) notes a dichotomy in social consciousness between the politics of work and the politics of community, a dichotomy that helps explain the patterns of political activity in Hartford.

> The centerpiece of these rules [of urban politics] has been the radical separation in people's consciousness, speech and activity of the politics of work from the politics of community. This subjective division has been such a powerful feature of American urban life that it has been operative even in situations where blue-collar workers live in immediate proximity to their factories. (6)

He contends that in the workplace, workers may respond as labor, but in their communities, working-class people define their identity in terms of race and territory. In other Western nations, mass-based left-leaning political parties have helped to bridge these two aspects of social life. But in the United States, the two-party system, the absence of mass parties, and American race relations all combine to produce a different set of political realities, notably a very muted politics of class in the electoral arena. Instead, urban politics tends to be defined by race or ethnicity and organized around patronage and services. This is all very evident in Hartford, as recent local political history illustrates.

The African American community in Hartford achieved several noteworthy electoral successes during the 1980s. In 1981, Thirman Milner was elected mayor, the first popularly elected African American mayor not only in Connecticut but in all of New England. While the post is not vested by the city charter with a significant degree of power within the city government, the mayor presides over council meetings and is highly visible in the city. The election of a Black mayor was an important source of racial pride for Hartford's African American community. To the rest of the city and the region, his election signaled the advent of a different power equation in the city.

After two successful reelection bids but with growing frustration over the limitations of the office, Milner chose not to seek reelection in 1987. The person he urged to seek election to replace him was successful, and another first took place in Hartford. Carrie Saxon Perry, an African American woman and several-term state representative, was elected mayor in 1987. Her election drew attention from both the national media and numerous national African American organizations.

The city council is the city's policymaking body. Since the Democratic members have an effective lock on six seats, they have great influence in setting policy goals and directives. But the city manager has a wide range of discretion in carrying out policy initiatives, particularly in budgetary matters, and is the individual to whom city departments are accountable. Under this arrangement there is a certain ambiguity of accountability. Community organizations or people with individual grievances sometimes take their concerns to council members, at other times they attempt to call on the city manager, or they may go to see the mayor.

Throughout the 1970s one person amassed a great deal of power on the council in the position of deputy mayor. Nicholas Carbone, celebrated by Clavel (1986) as a progressive policy leader, set the tone for Hartford's city government. He is credited with bringing together the public and private forces that began the revitalization of Hartford. The position of deputy mayor, the leader of the council selected by the majority party caucus, came to be regarded as the most powerful elected position in Hartford throughout the 1980s.

By 1979, Carbone's political hold was unraveling, and he was defeated in a hotly contested Democratic primary. During the next two raucous years, the position of deputy mayor was held by a maverick conservative Democrat, Robert Ludgin, who forged an alliance that included the city council Republicans as part of a voting majority. A degree of relative calm was restored in 1981, when Rudolph Arnold, an African American attorney who had served on the city council for the previous two years, was selected by a new Democratic caucus as deputy mayor, the first time the position of deputy mayor was held by an African American. Arnold was regarded by many in the city as extremely competent, intelligent, and easy to work with. Until 1989, however, the members of the "part-time" Hartford City Council were paid only $4,000 a year. (A 1989 referendum raised the remuneration to $15,000.) Arnold found it difficult to maintain his private legal practice and meet the heavy demands on his time that both council duty and the deputy mayor position required. In 1983 he chose not to seek reelection.

From 1983 until 1985, Francisco Borges, a business-oriented African American attorney, held the office of deputy mayor. He later became the treasurer for the state of Connecticut. From 1985 until 1989, the deputy mayor position was held by Alphonse Marotta, a former state employee union official from Hartford's heavily Italian South End. Neither man harnessed the same degree of power as had Carbone. Marotta eventually resigned and successfully sought a state assembly seat, and the deputy mayor position was assumed by council member I. Charles Matthews, an African American attorney for United Technologies. Matthews, staunchly procorporate and admittedly conservative, was defeated in a 1991 Democratic primary when his slate suffered a resounding loss to a slate of novice Democrats led by Carrie Perry.

In 1987 a new entity entered the political arena in Hartford. People for Change (PFC) constituted itself as a combination third party and community coalition. The group emerged from a battle for "linkage" waged by community organizations in which they pressed for some form of tax on downtown development to benefit the neighborhoods, and from dissatisfaction by labor unions over the council's inaction on the lengthy strike at Colt Firearms. Several forces joined in the coalition effort, including the Puerto Rican Political Action Committee and women's and gay rights organizations. Taking advantage of the state statute that guarantees minority party representation for three seats on the council, PFC presented a slate of three for city council as a third party in the November 1987 general election and captured two seats. They hoped to forge an alliance with other progressive council members in order to pursue a reform agenda, and they were aided in their campaigns by both disaffected Democrats and the Legislative Electoral Action Program (LEAP), an organization formed to provide technical assistance to progressive candidates. Marie Kirkley-Bey, a Black woman who was a respected neighborhood leader, and Eugenio Caro, a Puerto Rican community activist, were elected to the city council in the November 1987 election. William Hagan, the third candidate, became chairperson of PFC after his defeat.

In 1989, Kirkley-Bey decided to switch to the Democratic party, and for two years she fell in step with a closely controlled Democratic caucus. Sandra Little, an African American school social worker, and John Bonelli, Hartford's first openly gay candidate, ran with the incumbent Eugenio Caro in 1989. Little and Caro won but Bonelli lost, leaving one Republican, Roger Ladd, on the council. In 1991, however, the entire PFC slate of Caro, Little, and Louise Simmons (this author) was successful in winning office.

As the Puerto Rican community began to realize its political potential, its political leadership attempted to redefine their client status with the Democratic Town Committee of Hartford and develop a measure of independence from the existing political machine. In the mid-1980s the Puerto Rican Political Action Committee (PAC) was formed. The Puerto Rican PAC brought together leaders from diverse elements within the Puerto Rican community, including education, social service, business, and street-level activists. In 1987 when the PAC's choice for the city council slate was ignored by the Democratic Town Committee in favor of a less popular choice, the PAC threw its energy into the People for Change campaign, which accepted onto its slate the individual endorsed by the PAC, Eugenio Caro.

Even though the city council is elected at large by the voting public, the Democratic Town Committee attempted to "balance" the six-person slate it put forward through an equation that allocated positions based on a geographical, racial, and ethnic mix. Typically through the 1980s the slate's composition included two African American candidates; one Puerto Rican candidate who was seen to represent the entire Latino community; one candidate from the West End neighborhood—a liberal, racially mixed, but predominantly white, professional enclave—viewed as the "white liberal" of the council; and two South End candidates from what remains of more traditional white working-class areas of the city, one of whom was often Italian and the other Irish.

Throughout the 1980s any contesting slates in Democratic primaries mirrored this composition of the endorsed slate, and so the Democratic caucus on the city council was built on this equation of territory, race, and ethnicity. Female candidates were able to fill the slots if they also helped to balance the racial, ethnic, and territorial equation. Therefore, Hartford periodically has African American and Puerto Rican women as council members, as well as women of Italian, Irish, and other national origins. The ideologies represented by the African American members of the council have ranged from overtly procorporate council members to those with a more redistributive social service/legal service orientation.

An important postscript to this narrative is the electoral contest that took place after the research for this book was completed. In 1991, after a two-year term of escalating tensions with the Democratic city council members, Mayor Carrie Saxon Perry decided to assemble a council slate to challenge all six incumbents (including Kirkley-Bey). Her slate included two African Americans, two

Puerto Ricans, and two whites, showing a significant shift in power toward the Puerto Rican community. With agreement from People for Change to support her effort in a September primary in exchange for her support for the three-person PFC slate in November, an intense and emotional campaign brought her and her supporters an overwhelming victory. This tenuous effort at coalition politics effectively broke down during the 1991–1993 council term, portending more battles into the future. In 1993 Perry and three PFC candidates lost their election bids.

The composition of the city's delegation to the Connecticut House of Representatives has also generated intense contests, but within each of the respective districts. For example, from the early 1980s through the November 1988 election, Hartford sent to the capitol a seven-person delegation consisting of three Black representatives, four white representatives, and one Black state senator and one white state senator. Puerto Ricans grew increasingly impatient with their lack of representation, given the fact that Hartford has one of the largest (in relative terms) Puerto Rican populations in the continental United States. Bridgeport had a Puerto Rican representative for several years—the only Puerto Rican state representative in Connecticut—but Hartford had none.

The 1988 elections saw Hartford's Puerto Rican population organize intensely, resulting in Puerto Rican candidates' winning primaries in two districts and going on, in November, to take two of the seven seats. One of the victories was expected, and the other was a surprise to the entire city. One of the successful candidates replaced a white person, and the other replaced a Black person. In 1988, the city's delegation included two African Americans, two Puerto Ricans, and three whites in the state house, with one Black and one white in the state senate. Redistricting in 1990 incorporated several areas of the southern part of the city into previously all-suburban state house districts, bringing to nine the total number of representatives whose districts include Hartford. All are Democrats.

People for Change was the inspiration for the campaign of one of the victorious Puerto Rican representatives, Juan Figueroa. An attorney and activist in the Puerto Rican PAC, he participated in the 1987 PFC city council campaign effort, and spearheaded an effort to take control of his Town Committee through the vehicle of Democrats for Change (DFC). Figueroa's campaign was built on the technical expertise of People for Change and LEAP's methods of voter registration, targeting, and extensive telephone and door-to-door canvassing. He successfully challenged a several-term incumbent in the Democratic primary and went on to an easy victory in November.

Neighborhood Activism

By the late 1980s Hartford community activism revolved in large measure around constituency-based neighborhood organizations that derive their models and techniques from the Alinsky tradition of community organizing (see Alinsky 1946, 1971). Saul Alinsky, an organizer for the Congress of Industrial Organizations (CIO) during the 1930s and a confidante of John L. Lewis, fashioned a unique model of community organizing based on militant labor organizing techniques. The Alinsky model, harnessing grassroots energy and anger, is characterized by bold confrontational and often theatrical tactics. Alinsky's fearless and gutsy style has been emulated and adapted by several generations of community organizers in America. Fisher (1984) labels the modern movements in this tradition "neo-Alinskyism."

> The essence of neo-Alinskyism is to develop mass political organizations rooted in neighborhoods, grounded in local concerns, and focused on winning concrete gains. The goal is to advance social and economic democracy, empower people, and challenge power relations within and beyond the neighborhood. . . . All neo-Alinskyite projects employ the ideology of the new populism—decentralization, participatory democracy, self-reliance, mistrust of government and corporate institutions, empowering low- and moderate-income people—and

at best see themselves as grassroots organizations working to
connect up with the national political process. (133–34)

Neo-Alinskyism is to be distinguished from other forms of
community organizing that originated during the 1960s in that it is
not advisory, not generally tied to government funding or services,
and not necessarily focused on a specific issue. It is built instead on
the myriad concerns, often very simple but sometimes extremely
complex, that arise in local neighborhoods involving municipal
taxation structures and budgets or the practices of financial institutions.

In contrast to Alinsky's organizing endeavors in which he drew
on his CIO organizing experiences (Alinsky 1949) and implicitly
sought to overcome the gulf between the workplace and the
community, the staff and leadership of the neo-Alinsky organizations do not have prior associations with labor and employ Alinsky's model without the benefit of the experiences that inspired it.
The leadership of many of the newer neighborhood organizing
networks trace their roots to the era of student activism against the
war in Vietnam, when relationships between students and the
mainstream labor leadership were at best tenuous and often antagonistic. So, while perhaps seeking similar types of empowerment
goals for working-class populations, contemporary labor and
neighborhood organizing rely on very distinct methods and processes, a key distinction to which I return in detail.

Throughout the sixties and seventies various civil rights and local
civic and antipoverty organizations exerted influence as forces of
activism in Hartford. But the formation of the neighborhood
organizations and their subsequent successful development formal-
ized and, to some extent, institutionalized neighborhoods as key
bases of activism, and these groups in particular became the vehicles
for activism within the city.

The oldest of the three organizations, Hartford Areas Rally
Together (HART), formed in 1975. It defined its sphere of activity—its "turf"—as the southern half of the city, an area that has the

largest share of the white population. But that area also has a substantial Puerto Rican population and, in recent years, has seen a growing African American and Southeast Asian population. The initial financial backing for HART came from the Catholic Church's Campaign for Human Development. In recent years HART and the two other neighborhood organizations have secured United Way funding.

The southern half of the city contains several distinct neighborhoods. For planning purposes, the city of Hartford has designated eight residential neighborhoods and one commercial/industrial neighborhood in HART's turf. HART's neighborhood designations do not match exactly those of the city, and it does not organize in the public housing developments in the southern part of Hartford. But several areas are formally represented on HART's board of directors, along with an areawide senior citizens' organization and other issue-focused groups. In its early years HART appealed mainly to white homeowners. Later it attempted to set up an organization specifically for Hispanics, since that population was greatly increasing within HART's turf. After a problematic history, that organization eventually folded into HART's neighborhood-based organizations.

In the late 1980s, HART began to achieve a much more integrated membership, with some African American and Puerto Rican leadership. Although it is still significantly white in terms of members, leaders, and turf, it is a much different organization than it was when it was founded, especially in how it is perceived by the rest of the community. In its early years, there was curiosity and some suspicion in other neighborhoods in Hartford about what an organized South End would mean for the distribution of resources, services, and power. HART's organizing methodology consisted of setting up block clubs; a dedicated team of organizers was very successful in establishing over thirty clubs in the southern part of Hartford. Other neighborhoods began to look at HART's example as something to emulate. Two other organizations formed in the late 1970s and early 1980s.

Organized North Easterners–Clay Hill and North End, ONE-CHANE, is the product of a 1988 merger of two organizations. Clay Hill and North End, CHANE, served one of the most impoverished areas of Hartford from 1979 until 1988 and employed elements of the Alinsky model utilized by HART, as well as the more traditional civic association model. Its territory included an area with severe poverty, large public housing developments, massive welfare dependency, and every poverty-associated problem found in modern America. The population is almost entirely African American and Puerto Rican. CHANE itself grew out of loosely organized local neighborhood groups who came together around specific concerns. It received start-up funds from three insurance companies and later secured United Way and other types of funds. Organized North Easterners, ONE, operated as a small-scale community development organization in an adjacent area with significant homeownership and sections of middle-income populations. The impetus for ONE came from those residents with relatively higher (yet still modest) incomes in this neighborhood who were struggling to hold on to their homes and maintain their standard of living. In 1988 the two organizations merged, forming ONE-CHANE and attempting to build on both previous organizations' models.

Neighborhood organizing in the ONE-CHANE area has been among the most difficult and challenging in Hartford or, for that matter, anywhere else in the country. Families in some of these neighborhoods have suffered long-term poverty, and many of those who remain in the area have limited resources and limited opportunities for mobility.

The Asylum Hill Organizing Project (AHOP) was formed in 1983. Its turf is much more confined than HART's or ONE-CHANE's, but it operates in a dense, spottily gentrified, but mostly poor neighborhood. Asylum Hill is one of the highest-crime areas in Hartford, plagued with drug trafficking, transiency, prostitution, and other street-level problems. It is integrated, but mainly African American and Puerto Rican, and has a large elderly population.

Absentee slumlords have been a major problem in the neighborhood, and it has also undergone more condominium conversions than other areas in Hartford. Asylum Hill is home to Aetna Life and Casualty Insurance Company, Connecticut Mutual Insurance Company, St. Francis Hospital and Medical Center, St. Joseph's Cathedral (Hartford's only Catholic cathedral), and a number of other old, established churches. The churches assisted in AHOP's early development.

Asylum Hill's interesting history includes a residency by Samuel Clemens, who lived in this area when it was an artistic and literary enclave. The house he lived in, now known as the Mark Twain House, is one of Hartford's major tourist attractions. Today, the presence of two major insurance companies, particularly Aetna, gives the neighborhood a strategic importance that AHOP utilizes in its work.

Since 1983, AHOP's work has involved organizing tenants, building block clubs, developing neighborhoodwide coalitions on crime and other matters, working with local youth and seniors, and a host of other issues. AHOP has incorporated a social service center into its program and launched a housing development arm.

There are other smaller neighborhood-based organizations in Hartford, but the "Big Three" have the most stable resource bases, larger full-time staffs, and more day-to-day activities than any of the others. HART, AHOP, and ONE-CHANE are all members of a statewide network of neighborhood groups, United Connecticut Action for Neighborhoods (UCAN), which provides technical assistance and, in some instances, supervision of organizing staff for its member organizations.

The three groups also participate in National People's Action (NPA), one of four national networks of organizations employing neo-Alinsky methodologies. The other networks include ACORN (the Association of Community Organizations for Reform Now; analyzed by Fisher [1984] and Delgado [1986]); Citizen Action (associated with the Midwest Academy and Heather Booth); and the Industrial Areas Foundation (originally founded by Alinsky). Structure, relationships with local affiliates, positions on electoral politics, and emphases on strategies and tactics vary among the four networks. National People's Action (NPA) is the most loosely federated: It neither establishes nor gives direction to local or state organizations and has one annual national convention in Washington, D.C., during which time it stages demonstrations or activities at various federal departments. Reitzes and Reitzes (1987) assess NPA as the weakest national network and least sophisticated in terms of training or brokering national campaigns for reform. Local affiliates are characterized as "fiercely independent and unwilling to give up any local autonomy and so are hesitant to participate in any joint actions" (188). Fisher (1984) posits that NPA does not focus on electoral politics but instead adheres to the "pressure group model," convinced that electoral participation would undermine the grassroots effectiveness and quality of the organizations.

There is also an affiliate of the national Citizen Action network in Connecticut with a presence in Hartford, the Connecticut Citizens Action Group (CCAG). For a while CCAG established local neighborhood-based chapters. One existed in Hartford in the Blue Hills neighborhood in the early 1980s, but it ceased functioning after several years, and CCAG adopted a different organizing model with a more statewide focus.

The three neighborhood organizations command a distinct presence in the city in terms of public decision making and, in some cases, negotiating with private corporations over the impact of their policies or plans for the neighborhoods. These three groups are certainly among the best-organized and most grassroots-based local organizations. I examine in some detail various aspects of their methodologies—how they amass and wield power—and analyze the outcomes of several of their campaigns and other efforts.

The Labor Movement in Hartford

Workers in the Hartford area have experienced firsthand the painful impact of economic restructuring. Capital flight, deindustrialization, the emergence of low-wage service sector employment—

all elements of the new global economy—are no abstractions for workers in the city. The ripple effects (Bluestone and Harrison 1982) of tax-base erosion, municipal fiscal problems, unemployment and underemployment, small-business decline, lack of job security for individual workers, and other problems plague the urban environment. Organized labor, in particular, faces grim prospects: strikes, demands for concessions, plant closings, difficulties in maintaining membership and in organizing new members, and outright union-busting tactics on the part of employers. Still, workers and their unions carry on.

Hartford has a tradition of active labor unions, although the decline in union membership nationally is reflected in the city. Even so, close to ninety different union locals are currently affiliated with the Greater Hartford Labor Council, the local AFL-CIO body, representing between twenty-five thousand and twenty-eight thousand workers in the Hartford region. Since Connecticut is geographically compact and the unions involved in Hartford and the surrounding area operate statewide, it is useful to describe some of the larger unions in the state to better understand the context for the Hartford area labor movement.

The Connecticut State AFL-CIO consists of approximately 650 union locals and 170,000 members (Remez 1990). Two of the international unions with the largest statewide memberships include the International Association of Machinists (IAM), which represents workers at the United Technologies Pratt and Whitney Division plants in the state, at UTC's Hamilton Standard Division, and at several other employers in the state, and the American Federation of State, County and Municipal Employees (AFSCME), which represents a significant number of public employees, a large portion of whom are employed by the state of Connecticut.

The United Auto Workers (UAW) has represented thousands of workers in a variety of firms in the state since the 1950s, but in recent years the union has experienced a significant decline, from twenty-eight thousand in the early 1970s to less than half that number by the late eighties through plant closings and layoffs. Although affiliated nationally with the AFL-CIO, the UAW in Connecticut was not affiliated with the State Central Labor Council or the local labor councils until 1990, after decades of independent status. Several other unions are not affiliated with the state AFL-CIO body: The largest are the Teamsters locals in the state. In the Hartford area, a reform-minded leadership held office in one of the more sizable Teamster locals in the state during the late eighties, but was defeated in 1991 elections.

Two service sector unions have been among the most active in organizing new members: Hotel and Restaurant Employees (HERE) and the New England Health Care Employees Union–District 1199–Service Employees International Union. The aggressive, dedicated staffs of these unions possess a fierce commitment to their work and impart a militancy to the entire labor movement in the state, yet receive substantially lower salaries than staff members of other unions. District 1199 has over fifteen thousand members in Connecticut, approximately nine thousand of whom are employed by the state of Connecticut. It also represents the largely minority and female work forces at a number of nursing homes, community-based mental health clinics, and local hospitals throughout Connecticut. In the early 1980s, 1199 made headlines by simultaneously striking over fifteen nursing homes, using protest and garnering support from elected officials and civil rights organizations in the effort. In 1986 it waged a four-month strike at Waterbury Hospital. HERE has led several major strikes at hotels, including a three-month struggle in 1988 at the Hartford Sheraton, and also uses protest tactics and large support rallies to call public attention to its members' working conditions.

One of the most significant struggles in recent years for the labor movement in Hartford, and in Connecticut more generally, was a strike of over four years' duration at Colt Firearms with plants in Hartford and West Hartford. In January 1986, over one thousand workers walked off the job after working ten months without a contract. They were members of UAW Local 376, an amalgamated local that is one of the largest UAW locals in Connecticut and represents workers at over twenty different shops. The Colt membership is the largest bloc of members in Local 376.

Shortly after the strike began the union leadership met with the president of the Greater Hartford Labor Council and launched a strike support effort, the Community-Labor Alliance. The alliance played an important role in the strike: It organized periodic rallies, sponsored fund-raising activities, met with elected officials, and mounted other strike support activities during the Colt strike. Other strikes in the area were also assisted by the alliance, but clearly for labor in Connecticut and for other sympathetic forces, the Colt strike was a symbol of the harshest corporate treatment of workers in the era of economic restructuring. (The strike and the strike support effort are analyzed in more detail in later chapters.)

Many 1199 and HERE members and former Colt strikers live in neighborhoods that are also the turfs of AHOP, HART, and ONE-CHANE. District 1199 has hundreds of West Indian and African American members, mainly women, who live in the North End of Hartford, particularly the Blue Hills neighborhood. HERE members fill many of the service jobs in the restaurants and hotels downtown but cannot afford an overnight stay in the rooms they tend. They also live in Hartford's neighborhoods and are in large numbers African American and Latino residents. The former Colt strikers are a diverse group, including African American and Latino residents of Hartford. Some former Colt strikers are African American workers with as much as thirty-five to forty years' seniority—representing some of the most lucrative factory jobs for African Americans in Hartford. There are Puerto Rican former Colt strikers with fifteen to twenty years seniority. Many of the African American former strikers worked previously at Underwood or Royal and went to Colt when these factories closed.

Challenges for Labor and Neighborhood Organizing

Labor unions and neighborhood organizations face serious challenges in today's changing socioeconomic environment.

Labor Unions.   Union organizing is circumscribed by a complex legal framework, and unions as organizations are subject to numerous laws. In essence, the "rules" that govern their activities are not necessarily of their own making but the result of political processes rooted in the confluence of forces that led to the passage of the 1935 Wagner Act. The framework of American labor relations has changed considerably, however, as the economy has evolved since the thirties.

When the National Labor Relations Act was passed in 1935, the legal parameters outlined in the act reflected a public policy posture that conditionally accepted unions as legitimate participants in the economy: conditionally, as Tomlins (1985) notes, meaning as long as collective bargaining and the evolving system of U.S. labor relations contributed to industrial stability and labor peace. Collective bargaining became the preferred method of resolving labor-management conflicts, taking the place of the militant organizing drives that preceded World War II and the wave of strikes that followed the end of the war and eventually forced industrial leaders to accept unionization and agree to collective bargaining. Negotiation was preferable to unpredictable and disruptive strikes and rank-and-file actions.

In the post–World War II era and through the mid-1970s, management gained the right to control firms' investment and location decisions in exchange for union recognition, organizational security, and regular wage and working condition improvements tied to increases in productivity. During the early years of Pax Americana (Bluestone and Harrison 1982), McCarthyism helped quash labor militancy as Communist and radical elements were purged from union ranks, particularly from leadership roles.

Unions were accorded a "seat at the table" as long as their demands remained confined to the wage arena and as long as the leadership of the labor movement did not challenge the prevailing ideology embodied in the domestic and foreign policy of the country (Tomlins 1985; Montgomery 1979).

These features of the post–World War II system of industrial relations began to unravel during the economic restructuring of the mid-1970s. Organized labor has lost millions of members in recent years as American manufacturing has restructured, closed plants in this country, and moved operations to low-wage regions of the United States and overseas. Union growth has been exceedingly difficult, and many unions fear for their own survival as they face the combined threats of concessions, capital flight, overt union-busting campaigns, and the Reagan-Bush–era National Labor Relations Board, characterized by labor as decidedly promanagement. Moreover, job creation in the service sector has yet to translate into expanded union membership, although these workers are increasingly becoming targets of organizing drives.

An important aspect of the American industrial relations system is how union organizing occurs and how a work site changes upon being organized. The focus of a union organizing drive is very specific—employees in a particular firm or work site. The immediate goals include winning the right to represent a specific set of workers—usually through an NLRB-sponsored election—recognition of the union as the collective-bargaining agent by the employer, and a first contract. Once a work site becomes unionized, an entire new set of issues is presented, ranging from grievances and arbitration to future negotiations, from orienting and educating new members to preparing members for political action and the entire scope of other union activities. When strikes occur, the intense mobilization of workers that is required presents even greater challenges to a union. However, new organizing has also been made more difficult by the changing nature of both the workplace and the work force: With more and more employment creation in smaller businesses and with greater numbers of workers who have limited exposure to or previous affiliations with unions, unionization is not necessarily an "automatic" response on the part of workers facing problems. The labor movement has been plagued by negative public relations and perceptions.

Neighborhood Organizations. Unencumbered by the complex legal structure that circumscribes labor union activities in the United States, neo-Alinskyite neighborhood organizations are free to employ a variety of methods to achieve their goals. There are no legally prescribed sets of procedures that they must follow. The boundaries of a neighborhood are often not rigid, and there is no numerical majority of 51 percent that must be won in order to operate within a neighborhood. Moreover, there is no equivalent of a "union shop" for neighborhood organizations—membership is completely voluntary. Their targets are varied: landlords, financial institutions, political bodies, and corporations. However, these organizations encounter problems relating to unstable membership bases, restrictions from certain funders on political activities, revolving-door staffing patterns, and the inability to achieve objectives effectively (Fainstein and Fainstein 1985). Many neighborhood organizations are relatively young and do not analyze their successes and failures with an eye toward reformulation of their methodologies. Their practices may ignore racial and ethnic issues or concerns. As urban neighborhoods undergo rapid change in many cities, some analysts call for reexamining Alinsky-style organizing techniques in order to adapt to these new contours (McKnight and Kretzmann 1984).

Neo-Alinskyite organizations sometimes compete with other types of community organizations or with political organizations and parties. They are challenged to accommodate local cultures, to factor ethnic and racial traditions into their models of community organizing, and to fashion relationships with political leaders and forces. While they enjoy an immense degree of freedom in their choices of targets and strategies and in their relationships to legal processes and structures, they may also experience problems in focusing their work or in maintaining their ability to mobilize. Participants in neighborhood organizations may be pulled in competing directions in terms of time and energy devoted to the activities of their churches, their families, other local organizations, or basic survival.

The Exercise of Power.   In the post–World War II period, labor's power in the economic arena derived from its ultimate weapon, the strike, as a means of gaining wage increases and other improvements. It generally participated in politics as a partner in the Democratic party and derived political power by virtue of its numbers (Brecher and Costello 1988a). Given the national framework for labor relations described above, which obtained throughout the first three post–World War II decades, labor did not usually have to resort to political pressure and the creation of a favorable public opinion climate to achieve success in individual organizing drives or at the bargaining table.

Since the mid-1970s simply preserving past achievements has been extremely difficult for organized labor. To succeed in organizing or in collective bargaining, some unions have instituted political action programs at all levels of government and initiated new public relations strategies. In the contemporary climate, collective-bargaining demands are often difficult to win through withholding labor in a strike situation. Nowadays, unions are more likely to try to influence public opinion through such tactics as protest and civil disobedience.

The power of neighborhood groups, on the other hand, has generally been exercised at the local level and often focuses on the realm of public opinion. Tactics range from negotiation to protest and confrontation. Neighborhood groups rely heavily on protest tactics because they generally do not possess sufficient economic power to achieve their goals, and often their goals are not of a purely economic nature. The voluntary nature of their membership makes it difficult to define a solid base in the community, although protest tactics often help to create the impression of a large unified base.

Mutual Discovery.   In recent years a process of mutual discovery has been unfolding between labor and neighborhood organizations in various communities. The experiences vary from city to city and region to region. Often the nature of the local leadership has a great influence on the outcome of the process, but coalitions of trade unions and community and neighborhood organizations are now dotting the American landscape (Brecher and Costello 1988a, 1990). Sometimes in the context of difficult strikes in which labor needs community allies, at other times in the face of devastating plant closings, labor is reaching out beyond its own ranks to wage its struggles. Electoral coalitions, as well, are developing, and Connecticut offers several important examples that are analyzed in the next chapter. These coalitions and alliances constitute a new and emerging means of exercising power, and their potential is rapidly being recognized by the participants as a necessity in coping with the political and economic environment. Unless they are carefully nurtured, however, these coalitions can have very tenuous existences.

Commonalities.   Despite many differences in the contexts and the frameworks within which unions and constituency-based neighborhood organizations operate, there are certain common elements in their efforts. Both attempt to improve the living conditions of their members or constituents by redefining relations of power in their respective environments. These are the organizations that individuals turn to when they face a plant closing, a property tax hike, a gentrifying neighborhood, or a disciplinary action by a supervisor. Both types of organizations must overcome feelings of apathy and powerlessness and develop a sense of confidence within their members. Both rely on the power of numbers over the power of wealth, and to be at all successful, they must harness the collective power of individuals acting self-consciously to achieve goals.

In an introductory essay to Lee Staples's work on community organizing, *Roots to Power: A Manual for Grassroots Organizing,*

Cloward and Piven (1984) eloquently characterize some of the common elements that drive both types of organizations.

> Ordinary people have always been moved to political action in the local settings where they live and work. It is in the local settings that people come together in solidarity groups, where they discover common grievances, and where they sometime find sources of institutional power. What people can do is a reflection of their particular objective circumstances: as workers, they can withhold labor; as tenants, they can withhold rent; as savers, they can withhold savings; as consumers, they can withhold purchases; and, as citizens, they can withhold obedience to the rules governing civil society. . . . Whether people band together as tenants, workers, minority group members, women, or environmental and peace activists, it is their neighborhoods, factories, housing projects and churches that provide the nexus for mobilization. Terminology should not mislead us. In this respect, community organizing is not different from other efforts to organize popular political power. And that has always been so, no matter the moment in history when popular mobilization erupted. (xiv)

This book is an attempt to understand the generic nature of organizing and the forms it assumes in the spheres of work and community within the context of economic restructuring. Not only do the capacities of community organizations and labor unions to motivate and engage individuals in collective action figure critically in the processes and outcomes of economic restructuring, but the survival of both kinds of organizations hinges on their respective effectiveness. In the chapters that follow I tell the stories of Hartford's neighborhood organizations and unions as they adjust to economic restructuring. I focus on three neo-Alinskyite organizations and three of the area's most activist unions. My examination of innovative techniques in organizing, electoral participation, and coalition activities helps to reveal barriers between the politics of work and the politics of community—formidable obstacles in any collaboration. Understanding the nature of these barriers sheds light on the difficulties involved in fashioning cohesive responses to restructuring.

I concentrate on the period 1987 to 1990 in Hartford and, when appropriate, comment on subsequent developments. That period in Hartford offered new challenges in the arenas of labor organizing, neighborhood organizing, electoral work, and coalition building. I was fortunate to be a part of many activities and to have access to many key actors and organizations. There are few studies that examine critical economic and social phenomena from the perspectives of grassroots organizing and internal functioning of unions. These stories need to be told both to more deeply understand social change and to allow the organizers and organizations room to analyze their successes and failures.

By first examining the coalition and electoral experiences in Hartford—the outermost layers of the groups' practices—I set the stage for a discussion of the internal logic and innovations in methodology, in local labor organizing and neighborhood organizing. In examining the two forms of collective action, however, I want to highlight the most relevant features of the respective methodologies and not to offer a point-by-point comparison. For the labor unions it is possible to see their work in terms of three aspects: organizing new members, working with existing members, and dealing with organizational maintenance issues. But for the neighborhood organizations there is not a ready distinction between organizing new members and mobilizing existing memberships, and therefore I focus on two aspects of their work: participants and issues, and organizational maintenance issues.

The Colt strikers' stake in their jobs and their union and the community's stake in maintaining the jobs found expression in the Community-Labor Alliance. The experiences of the Colt strikers and their supporters in the alliance, and other coalition efforts such as People for Change, show how labor and neighborhood organizing methods and philosophies confront each other and potentially influence how communities and individuals cope with economic change.

Alliances, Coalitions, and Electoral Activities

During the late 1980s, an array of coalitions and electoral activities emerged locally in Hartford and statewide in Connecticut. Ranging in focus from single issues to strike support, from electoral initiatives to information sharing, these activities and coalitions have been national models for activists and analysts of progressive social movements (see Shapiro 1986; and Brecher and Costello 1988a, 1988b, 1990). They had a quality of building on and reinforcing each other that allowed members of different organizations to call on each other for support. The discussion below lists examples of situations in which neighborhood organizations and unions became either directly or indirectly involved with each other. In some instances they formed coalitions based on specific issues and in other instances they worked together in electoral coalitions.

The Linkage Coalition. Initiated by the neighborhood groups in the mid-1980s and receiving support from several unions, this coalition lobbied the Hartford City Council to adopt a policy of taxing downtown development projects in order to generate funds for housing and job development. The issue came to a head in 1986 when the Democratic council majority at the time, who had run for office on a prolinkage platform, voted down the measure. Along with financial and business interests, the building trade unions lobbied heavily to oppose the effort, causing tremendous alienation on the part of the neighborhood organizations toward labor.

The Community-Labor Alliance (for strike support) (CLA). In January 1986, when one thousand members of UAW Local 376 struck Colt Firearms in Hartford, the union and the Greater Hartford Labor Council initiated the effort. Neighborhood organizations, other unions, political leaders, segments of local clergy, and other activists participated in scores of CLA-sponsored activities throughout the lengthy strike. Other unions came to the CLA for strike support and other forms of assistance.

Anticrime Coalitions. Each of the neighborhood groups deals extensively with ever-rising crime rates. For the first year of the Colt strike, police resources were deployed in force to the picket line. The union local, the Community-Labor Alliance, several neighborhood organizations and other community organizations came together to demand reduced police deployment at the strike and redeployment into the neighborhoods. The effort was partially successful in reducing the number of police at the Colt gate, but the neighborhood demand for better police protection continued. Neighborhood organizations also formed a coalition demanding the assignment of police foot patrols to neighborhood beats in Hartford and specifically countered the police department's strategy of pitting one group against the other by the simultaneous presentation of similar demands from each organization.

Grassroots-Labor Forum. In 1987, the president of the Greater Hartford Labor Council initiated monthly meetings with the neighborhood organizations to share information on their respective activities. The effort was undertaken to open lines of communication after the divisive linkage battle.

Legislative Electoral Action Program (LEAP). LEAP was initiated in 1980 as a statewide progressive electoral coalition comprising political action committee representatives from over twenty different unions, as well as consumer, women's, environmental, civil rights, and community organizations. LEAP makes political endorsements, trains campaign workers, and marshals resources to assist candidates. It has an impressive track record of developing successful campaigns for candidates seeking office in the Connecticut state legislature. LEAP-backed state senators and state representatives formed a Progressive Caucus in the state legislature and have attempted to promote a progressive agenda within the legislature. Region 9A of the UAW hired its first director to help develop similar coalitions in other states in the Northeast, and the model is being implemented in New England and elsewhere.

People for Change (PFC). As described in the previous chapter, PFC emerged out of dissatisfaction with the Hartford City Council on the linkage issue, on its response to the Colt strike, and on other issues. PFC constituted itself as a third party and ran a slate of three candidates in the 1987 race for city council. It sought to replace the three Republicans on the nine-member at-large council whose election had been guaranteed by a state statute prohibiting political parties from nominating slates to fill more than two-thirds of the seats on at-large bodies. PFC receives technical support from LEAP in its campaigns. PFC ran a second three-person slate in 1989. In both of these elections two of the three candidates won contests. In 1991 all three PFC candidates won. It lost its seats in 1993.

It is important to mention one additional example: In September 1987 UAW Region 9A sponsored "Working Together and Winning—A Progressive Policy and Coalition Strategy Conference" held at the Walter and May Reuther Family Education Center at Black Lake, Michigan. The regional leadership of the UAW in New England held this conference for both UAW members and invited guests from other unions, community groups, women's and peace organizations, as well as progressive elected officials from throughout New England, parts of New York, and Puerto Rico. The UAW paid lodging and travel expenses for all of the several hundred participants. Similar conferences were held in November 1989, October 1991, and November 1993.

Other coalitions in Hartford have brought together even more diverse groupings, some involving one or more unions or neighborhood organizations. Examples include Jesse Jackson's presidential campaign in 1988, a coalition supporting the school desegregation lawsuit *Sheff v. O'Neill* in Connecticut, a campaign to extend health insurance to the uninsured, and senior citizen issue coalitions.

Within these coalitions the methodologies of unions and the neo-Alinsky neighborhood organizations have confronted each other in various ways. Three aspects of coalitions help illustrate the issues and difficulties: rationales for involvement, experiences within coalitions, and coalition outcomes. The Community-Labor Alliance and the early years of People for Change are rich with examples.

RATIONALES FOR INVOLVEMENT

Although coalitions and alliances take many forms, generally an organization enters into a coalition because it cannot achieve a particular goal on its own. Therefore, a coalition effort is a tacit recognition of the capacities and limits of each organization. Coalitions may also serve to mediate potential conflicts among members: They can be a forum for working out competing interests and claims. For example, among other activities, the AFL-CIO—the largest coalition of labor unions in the country—serves both to marshal the collective resources of its member unions in such areas as political action and to mediate disputes between unions. Through its highly formal organizational structure, it mediates jurisdictional conflicts arising from the process of organizing new members and it sanctions violators. When unions affiliate with the AFL-CIO, they simultaneously strengthen the collective voice of labor, gain certain benefits they could not achieve individually, and agree to abide by various rules and procedures.

For many unions, participation in the AFL-CIO is their major coalition activity. The AFL-CIO operates on national, state, and local levels with various activities at each level. Through the mid-1970s many unions might have found this form of coalition activity sufficient. Some segments of the labor movement participated in the civil rights movement and the Vietnam War–era peace movement, and several unions framed their organizing drives as extensions of the civil rights movement (significant examples include the United Farmworkers and the Hospital Workers Union–

Local 1199—see Fink and Greenberg 1989). As a whole, however, the labor movement did not often reach out beyond its own ranks. But as the framework of industrial relations began to change in the 1970s, some unions began to look outside labor's ranks for assistance (Brecher and Costello 1988a, 1988b, 1990). In Hartford, this general pattern also obtained, and the coalition work of recent years represents new directions for the segments of the labor movement involved.

During the Reagan era and particularly in the late 1980s, coalition work became more acknowledged as an important avenue for promoting labor's agenda. Perhaps the massive mobilization in September 1981 for the Solidarity Day demonstration in Washington, D.C., can be seen as the beginning of the new era—the exact date or year may be arguable—but the 1980s witnessed a new pattern of coalition building across the entire country (Brecher and Costello 1990). In the Hartford area, Region 9A of the UAW had experienced a severe decline in membership because of plant closings. When the Colt strike began in 1986, the UAW immediately decided to call for a strike support coalition, realizing that without community support, the strike effort would be nearly impossible. In concert with the Greater Hartford Labor Council, whose president wanted both to support the strike effort and to develop stronger ties with community organizations, the Community-Labor Alliance was launched.

Among the first groups sought for participation were the three constituency-based neighborhood organizations, AHOP, HART, and ONE-CHANE. Labor leaders were impressed with the organizing abilities of the neighborhood groups and recognized their grassroots base in the community. The labor council president also realized that the posture of the building trades unions in the linkage issue created an immense public relations problem for labor. This negative image could impede new organizing drives and create a pool of replacement workers in strike situations: neighborhood residents who had never been union members and who would harbor resentment against unions. Moreover, many Colt strikers

and, as it turned out, replacement workers lived in the neighborhoods that the three organizations claimed as their "turfs."

So for unions facing problematic situations, organizational interests may call for the formation of alliances and coalitions. Unions
that are vulnerable to plant closings, to concessionary bargaining
that can force difficult strikes, and to a general climate of union
busting often choose to look outside their ranks for support.
Neighborhood organizations, however, may not feel that same
degree of vulnerability. In Hartford, they tend to approach coalition
efforts more pragmatically, as specific tactical choices rather than as
a larger strategy for survival. Neighborhood groups have a different
sense of the importance of coalitions for several reasons: They are
younger as organizations, they have not felt the same type of assault
in recent years as unions have, and they have very different bases of
membership. They face the constant challenge of issue-by-issue
organizing and mobilizing. They have no equivalent of a "union
shop," and any issue may draw new constituents into the work of
the organization. But since the terms of membership are completely
voluntary, a major portion of organizational resources is devoted to
these base-building activities. Coalition work may dilute an already
tenuous base and drain resources and loyalties.

The neighborhood groups are also drawing on a much shorter
history of experiences and traditions. In the labor movement, the
concept of "union solidarity" still resonates, and despite at times
tense interunion rivalries, it is a value orientation invoked to
mobilize support activities. The neighborhood organizations have a
much less clearly defined and developed sense of mutual support. By
nature and definition they are turf-oriented and center their activities on a particular geographical area. This concept of "localism"
(Fisher 1984) as an organizing principle may contribute to placing
a more limited value on coalitions, except in situations in which
other neighborhood organizations are working simultaneously on
similar issues.

Both District 1199 and Hotel and Restaurant Employees (HERE)
attach different meanings and significance to coalition endeavors

than the UAW does, and both echo some of the same concerns about coalitions as the neighborhood groups. Both engage in coalitions and use outside supporters in strikes and organizing drives, but they emphasize their respective internal strengths and their ability to win contests. The leaders of both feel that the major function of their organizations is to develop the ability to empower workers to take on employers, and therefore coalition work is somewhat secondary. The leaders of 1199 recognize the importance of coalitions and the need to join with other organizations to achieve various goals because of the low level of unionization in this country. But the president also believes that the further away the union moves from "shop floor" issues, the more potential there is for division among the membership.

While both 1199 and HERE generally do not face the problems of capital flight, they do face problems related to representing workers in industries that are subject to complicated and fluctuating financial problems. The crisis state of the U.S. health care system places a particularly difficult burden on a union that has many members in the lower-paying jobs of the industry. Hotels and especially restaurants change owners and managers frequently or close suddenly. Neither union possesses enough power in its respective industry to shut down significant portions of that industry, as, for example, does the UAW with domestic auto producers. In the health care sector, public opinion backlash is also a factor 1199 must consider. Therefore, even though they are more selective about their involvements, alliances and coalitions play important roles in the struggles of 1199 and HERE.

The rationales for political involvement are likewise quite divergent among the organizations. Unions in Hartford have historically participated fairly routinely in electoral activities, generally within the Democratic party, although occasionally some unions have endorsed Republican candidates. Both the UAW and 1199 are extremely active in politics, especially in LEAP's attempt to develop and maintain a progressive presence and direction within the Democratic party. In the case of 1199, which represents state health care workers as well as workers in state-regulated health care settings (hospitals, nursing homes, and private nonprofit subcontractors with the state of Connecticut), political involvement in state legislative contests is seen as critical to winning better contracts and working conditions. Many members see clearly the connection between who is elected to office and the policies that affect them on the job, and they therefore participate actively in elections. District 1199 also involves itself vigorously in elections for the U.S. Senate and House of Representatives and was the major force among labor for Jesse Jackson's 1988 presidential campaign in the Hartford area.

Through its Community Action Program (CAP) Councils, the UAW is involved in all types of elections, since its members may be affected by policies formulated at all levels of government. John Flynn, previous regional director of Region 9A (which includes New England, parts of New York, and Puerto Rico), was a Democratic National Committee member for many years as well as the president of LEAP, and the UAW in the area has a strong tradition of activism within the Democratic party. Its leadership feels that political involvement is essential to their goals.

HERE's political involvement once more seems to resemble the neighborhood organizations in that it has tended not to get heavily involved in elections, but does maintain access to officeholders and politicians. As with other forms of coalition activity, they attach more importance to their internal issues than to significant involvement in electoral campaigns. While they issue endorsements, they do not regularly participate in LEAP or PFC because of limited financial and other resources. They did launch a voter registration drive in 1989 and tend to become involved in electoral activities when they feel clearly that their interests are served.

AHOP, HART, and ONE-CHANE as organizations are not involved in electoral politics, because much of their funding is contingent on their nonprofit, nonpartisan status. Entering the arena of electoral politics would jeopardize this critical resource base, including funding from the United Way of the Capitol Region, an unusual accomplishment for Alinksy-style organizations. Yet, there is another important aspect to their lack of participation in electoral politics. Much of the leadership, especially full-time staff members, are committed to an antielectoral stance for their organizations in the belief that neighborhood organizations are more effective if they remain outside the electoral arena and operate as independent pressure groups to hold public officials accountable. The organizers state that they do not want their organizations to be viewed as partisan or as a stepping-stone for political aspirants and they want to avoid the internal tensions that might result from engagement in electoral politics, especially at the local level. Races for municipal office involve huge efforts in canvassing neighborhoods on a house-by-house basis. Divisions within a specific neighborhood over who to support could potentially translate into divisions within the neighborhood organization if it embraced political campaigns. Despite this organizational orientation, many individuals who are active in the three groups are also very involved in local politics, and sometimes the lines tend to blur between the different roles of these individuals.

The existence of neighborhood organizations encourages the emergence of candidates who represent the views of those organizations, as was the case in the People for Change experience. What happens in this political climate is quite beyond the direct control of the neighborhood groups: They may or may not agree with the directions pursued by organizations who attempt to articulate their issues within the political arena. Moreover, the existence of a political organization like PFC tends to dilute their raisons d'être: Now there are politicians from the ranks of neighborhood organizations attempting to work through political parties to achieve ends similar to those of the neighborhood organizations. Yet, even without the formal trappings of a political party such as endorsements or party processes, the Hartford neighborhood groups constitute a political force by virtue of the public opinion climate they create and its subsequent impact on city government.

EXPERIENCES WITHIN COALITIONS

Coalitions inevitably create situations in which the distinct styles and processes of the organizations involved confront each other and the different perspectives in each arena become apparent. Both in the Community-Labor Alliance and in People for Change, during its formative months, some of these differences caused tensions in the functioning of the coalitions. Several issues surfaced in only one coalition experience and others in both. The problems tend to be interrelated and, in combination, represent some of the most immediate difficulties in attempting to unite unique organizations into coalitions.

The Community-Labor Alliance and the Colt Strike

In the CLA, during the initial months of the strike, meetings were held every week, with as many as thirty to forty people attending. Members of several unions, community organizations, and the three neighborhood organizations attended. Initially the participation of the neighborhood groups was regular, then became sporadic, and eventually ceased, although they remained available for specific strike support activities. Neighborhood organizers highlighted a number of issues that probably contributed to the declining participation of the neighborhood organizations in the CLA. These relate to agenda formation and decision-making processes, leadership roles, relationships to legal processes, applying pressure and exerting power, and the question of "ownership," or stakeholding, in an issue.

Agenda Formation and Decision-Making Processes.   When neighborhood organizations decide to form a coalition, as was the case in the Linkage Coalition, the first actual meeting is preceded by careful negotiations to insure the equal participation of all organizations. No single organization dominates: Meeting sites and chairpersons are rotated. Agenda items involve specific planning and task assignments. Decisions are arrived at through a process of consensus development—a gradual unfolding of agreement through discussion without formally voting on issues through parliamentary procedure. These issues of process are as important as the substantive issues that necessitate the coalition's formation. This task-orientation and consensus development method is quite different from the way the CLA operated.

Within the CLA a tacit understanding developed that the UAW had the ultimate authority in decision making on issues related to the Colt strike. During the strike the UAW leadership was receptive to suggestions and planning from non-UAW members, but if the union leadership felt that a particular suggestion conflicted with its overall approach, the plan was not adopted. Other unions who came to the CLA for support in strike situations likewise held veto power over suggestions or plans developed in the meetings. The decision making was informal and consensual and, as in the neighborhood organizations' coalitions, generally did not involve formal voting. However, the specific union whose strike or issue was discussed had to be supportive of any plans undertaken with respect to its issue.

The major portion of the CLA agenda revolved around the Colt strike during its four years. In the first year of the strike there was an urgency about carrying out plans. As time passed, however, a sense developed among CLA participants that meetings might go on indefinitely and the urgency to accomplish tasks within a short time frame diminished. Some plans were never followed through to conclusion. This indeterminacy could easily frustrate the neighborhood group participants who engage in coalitions with a much more immediate and instrumental orientation.

Leadership Roles.   One major difference between the two types of organizations is the definition and use of leadership. Elected union officers are generally the full-time functionaries of the union and are constitutionally vested with the authority to make and execute many decisions. The actual titles may vary—president, business agent, secretary-treasurer—and the internal structures of unions may differ, but there are clearly elected union officials, often employed full-time by the organization. Even rank-and-file groups who might be opposed to existing leadership function within this framework.

The leadership of the neighborhood groups, however, can be described as shared to a great extent between the staff and elected leaders. The full-time staff of neighborhood organizations are not the elected leaders—they are usually hired by a board of directors consisting of volunteer citizen leaders. Citizen leaders from the respective neighborhoods are elected to the positions of president and other offices at annual neighborhood congresses, but they often are employed full-time elsewhere and participate in the neighborhood organizations as volunteers during their leisure time. So when the full-time staff of these organizations are contacted about specific plans or actions, they generally check with the elected citizen leaders and work through committees to make decisions. Within the CLA experience, this situation caused some frustration to the labor participants when they attempted to involve the neighborhood organizations and were not able to get ready responses to requests for assistance or participation.

Relationships to Legal Processes.   A critical difference between the two types of organizations that has an impact on coalitions derives from the organizations' respective relationships to legal processes and attorneys. Much of modern labor relations is bound by laws, precedents, and legal interpretations. In the Colt strike, the UAW sought to have the strike legally designated as an unfair-labor-practices strike by the NLRB. This strategy involved the union's filing charges with the NLRB alleging unfair labor practices on the part of the company, the NLRB's conducting a trial before an administrative law judge on the merits of the charges, and if the union prevailed, the NLRB could order reinstatement and back pay for the strikers. The point of this strategy is to prove that the company caused and may have prolonged the strike by its illegal actions. An unfair labor practices strike is afforded a legal status different from that of an economic strike. In an economic strike, one in which workers strike over wages or working conditions without formally alleging unfair labor practices by the employer, there is no legal route to pursue reinstatement. Replacement workers who are hired during the strike may be retained by the company once the strike is over, unless a settlement mandates otherwise. But in an unfair labor practices strike, the NLRB may mandate reinstatement and back pay for the strikers.

This brief outline of the unfair labor practice strike strategy does not begin to describe the legal complexities, the lengthiness of the process, and the ways in which employers can and do respond. In the Colt strike the company hired replacement workers, offering them permanent jobs—a strategy that polarized the situation and complicated the company's position in the NLRB trial, particularly in the event of a union victory and a mandate from the board to reinstate the strikers. Colt had also filed unfair labor practices against the union, alleging picket line misconduct. Although in 1989 Colt Industries decided to sell the Firearms Division, it could still be liable for back pay if the UAW won the trial. This liability figured significantly in the final sale of the company.

The activities of the CLA were limited by the decision of the UAW leadership not to pursue any strategy that would jeopardize the case at the NLRB. Therefore they usually discussed their plans with legal counsel before pursuing particular strategies, even if labor law was not specifically involved. The union leadership was not opposed to militant or innovative tactics as long as those tactics did not jeopardize their overall game plan.

Neighborhood organization members and staff were frustrated by the UAW's reliance on the opinions of attorneys. They have a strong aversion to such reliance on lawyers: They are much freer than unions to create their own rules, and their activities are not so circumscribed by laws and legal procedures. Except where absolutely necessary, they avoid ceding control to outside forces such as courts.

Applying Pressure and Exercising Power.   The two types of organizing confronted each other in the CLA in the planning and carrying
out of several demonstrations at the home, in Vernon, Connecticut, of the former president of Colt Firearms Division, Gary
French, in 1986 and 1987. The first demonstration took place
in July 1986 and was organized as a children's vigil, with children
of the strikers and supporters delivering pleas to French to settle
the strike. Several subsequent demonstrations during that summer focused on the plight of the strikers and urged French to
intervene to settle the strike. French himself did not participate
in negotiations, and, before the demonstrations, he was not featured in press accounts of the strike. Instead, the company's
vice-president for labor relations represented the company in formal negotiations.

The plans for the demonstrations were formulated within the
CLA after a consensus developed to take the strike beyond the
picket line and negotiations for symbolic reasons and to refocus
the situation on one person, Gary French. The object was to make
French the target, and the tactics borrowed heavily from Alinsky-
style methodologies typically used against slumlords.

The CLA planned activities at French's residence and elsewhere
in his local community. But these plans were interrupted in the fall
of 1986 when French went to court to invoke a 1947 Connecticut
statute that barred picketing at company officials' residences during
labor disputes, unless the residences were adjacent to work sites.
The CLA had been aware of the statute but characterized the
demonstrations as vigils rather than picketing, and the UAW was
prepared in any event to challenge the constitutionality of the law.
In October 1986, an injunction was issued barring demonstrations
at French's home. The UAW engaged legal counsel to appeal the
injunction to the Connecticut Supreme Court, and in May 1987, the
statute was declared unconstitutional. Between September 1986
and June 1987, all plans for demonstrations in Vernon were put on
hold. After the Supreme Court decision, French served notice that
he was going back to court to obtain punitive damages and an

injunction barring demonstrations at his residence, this time basing his actions on invasion of privacy.

In the interim between the May 1987 Supreme Court decision and the court date for the second injunction in late July 1987, the CLA and the UAW considered various alternatives. Since during that approximate two-and-a-half month period no injunction was in effect barring demonstrations, they were free to hold one. The UAW met with the Vernon Police Department to work out a set of guidelines for demonstrations. A draft agreement between the UAW and the Vernon Police Department was presented to the CLA at its June 10, 1987, meeting. The discussions at that meeting and at the subsequent June 17, 1987, meeting illustrate some of the different models and logics used by the union leaders and neighborhood organizers.

The neighborhood organizing viewpoint emphasized the strategy of keeping the target, French, guessing about the group's next move, not playing into the hands of the company or French by holding the expected demonstration, and also not submitting to externally determined rules (the UAW–Vernon Police Department agreement). Other types of actions aimed at French were suggested. The discussion at the June 10 meeting emphasized that by submitting to an agreement with the police, other organizations in the future may be forced into similar agreements against their wishes. Moreover, the argument went, such an agreement ceded power and control to an outside force. The point was to keep control of the situation within the CLA and to keep French off balance. Several unionists outside UAW 376 and one UAW 376 staff member agreed with this viewpoint. Another UAW 376 staff member, himself an attorney and party to the negotiations with the Vernon Police Department, argued that the draft agreement actually stretched conventional legally defined conditions of demonstrating in residential areas. Still others argued that since the effort had been made to overturn an unconstitutional law, the group should exercise its hard-won right to demonstrate. The majority of the UAW leadership at the meeting took the position that holding demonstrations at

French's house would show the union's strength against the company and boost the morale of the strikers. Since the UAW was in the process of preparing for the NLRB trial, the leadership was eager to take advantage of the victory but cautious about pursuing any strategies or tactics that might damage its credibility with the NLRB.

At the June 17 meeting of the CLA, a lengthy plan was presented for a campaign to pressure Gary French, based on the premise that he could make the decision to settle the strike and that with enough pressure on him as an individual, he would make that decision. While the general contours of the plan were accepted by the group, some participants' acceptance was based on the view that any publicity would be helpful in swaying public opinion in favor of the strikers and that such activities would boost the sagging morale of the strikers after eighteen months on the picket line. Community organizer Rick Kozin and labor organizer Steve Thornton (also a community activist), who fashioned the plan, believed that this strategy could ultimately win the strike.

These discussions underscored the differences in the styles and objectives of organizing in the two arenas. The UAW in the Colt strike had pursued a legal strategy from the outset and had conducted this strike within the context of the legal parameters defined by labor law. The UAW leadership felt that by carefully building a compelling case, the NLRB would have no choice but to find in favor of the union. The UAW was playing by rules—the conventions of the American labor law system—to which it felt there were no viable alternatives. Faced with the opportunity to hold the Vernon demonstration, they were inclined to enter into negotiations with the police department over the terms and conditions of such a demonstration. The experience of the union and the manner in which it conducted its business lent itself to such an approach to problem solving.

In contrast, the neighborhood organizing model is not dependent upon legally defined methods of resolving disputes. Neighborhood organizers do not put faith in legal strategies as a means to victory and caution members about relying on such strategies. Moreover, since the targets of these groups often are individuals, strategies can be built upon the premise that pressure upon one individual is sufficient to achieve success. The plan to pressure French did not conform to any externally created rules, and control of the situation rested with the CLA and UAW. If it could be successful, the strategy would be an innovative way to approach a strike. Moreover, the locus of activity would be moved away from the industrial setting and into the larger community.

The UAW leadership was receptive to the plan presented on June 17, 1987, even though its overall strategy was clearly bound by labor law. Several factors might explain this. First, they recognized in the beginning of the strike that it would be lengthy and would require the imaginations and resources of forces beyond its usual base to maintain the effort. They also saw the response to this strike as part of the nationwide effort to bust unions and believed that other unions and community groups would realize the stakes involved and could be rallied to its cause. They were open to innovative strategies, as long as final decisions rested within the UAW.

Second, in pursuing a legal strategy, the UAW had to restrain its members on the picket line from physically attacking the strike-breakers. Should its members engage in overt violence, the NLRB case would be jeopardized. However, the animosity toward the company and especially the strikebreakers had to find expression, and the president of the company made a perfect target. Pursuing French could offer a means of venting anger for the strikers. Some of the tactics could actually be fun for the strikers and afford a little comic relief.

Third, this could provide an opportunity for publicity. The human aspect of the strike as expressed in the original children's vigil created negative publicity for the company and sympathy for the strikers. If carefully planned and executed, the campaign to pressure Gary French would not necessarily endanger the other strategies the union was pursuing.

In this situation, the union's agenda and the neighborhood organizing methods could eventually converge, despite the very different ways in which each type of organization perceived the opportunities and had operated previously. For the union, this would be one more method of attempting to win a very difficult strike.

Ultimately, very little of the Gary French campaign was actually implemented. As other issues arose and as the work required to implement the plan appeared complex and time-consuming, enthusiasm for it dwindled. A demonstration was held at the home of Gary French, however, before the July 1987 court date. It was orderly, the union cooperated with the police, and French's second attempt at an injunction and punitive damages failed. During the summer of 1988 yet another demonstration was held at French's home at the conclusion of the lengthy NLRB trial.

Ownership of Issues and Stakeholding.   One final, very important aspect of the CLA experience and the participation of the neighborhood organizations in the effort has to do with the sense of ownership of an issue. The neighborhood groups perceived the strike as the UAW's issue or labor's issue—an important issue, but not their issue in the same way that they had embraced the linkage struggle as their issue. They did not embrace the strike as a communitywide issue with implications for the entire area, as did other unions in the region. Since their staff had little familiarity or involvement with unions and since most of the citizen leaders have limited experience with unions, the implications of a strike are not readily apparent to neighborhood activists. During the Colt strike, many began to see commonalities between their neighborhood work and labor's mission in the workplace, but they found it difficult to devote scarce resources, particularly human resources, to the strike support effort. As time has passed since the conclusion of the strike and with constant turnover in both neighborhood organization staff and local leadership, the lessons from the strike seem to be fading.

People for Change

In the launching and subsequent development of People for Change, efforts to coalesce neighborhood and labor forces and build a long-term agenda were hampered by inability of neighborhood organizations to participate and by differences in perception of the purpose of PFC and the nature of organizations' participation.

Decision-Making Processes Revisited.   The initial PFC conveners in early 1987 included the immediate past president of one of the neighborhood organizations, other individuals who had been active in the linkage issue, and several labor leaders, Puerto Rican activists, and activists in other arenas. They initially met to discuss participation in the upcoming city council election that year (1987). The first meeting produced no conclusions or strategies except an agreement to continue to meet and to expand the number of participants. For several months the group considered and debated different strategies, all the while with new participants entering the process.

Debate focused on whether or not to work within the Democratic party and field a slate of candidates in a primary against the incumbent council members or to field a slate of independent third-party candidates, and how many people might be on such a third-party slate. The process was lengthy and tedious. Eventually the group settled on the third party strategy, uncharted territory for everyone involved. Throughout, no one wanted to move too quickly and risk alienating a segment of the evolving coalition. Rather than putting many matters to a vote early on and generating polarized voting blocs, the discussion and the process dragged on.

Union leaders were frustrated with the indecision and with the inefficiency of constantly rehashing issues. They were used to being able to come to a decision, vote, and move forward with a plan of action, but the convening chairperson followed the consensus model of conducting meetings, which required devoting a large amount of attention and time to process issues. Once the group came to a decision and selected the slate of candidates, process issues ceased being very important, and a campaign mode of operation took over.

PFC's electoral campaign was managed by an experienced campaign manager from the LEAP staff. Precise voter targeting, voter registration campaigns, extensive telephone and door-to-door canvassing, constant fund-raising activities, and large numbers of volunteers devoting hundreds of hours all were coordinated by a team of LEAP-trained activists and staff members. The campaign mode resembled more of a command structure than the participatory, loosely coordinated coalition of the previous six months, and some resentment developed among several PFC activists at the atmosphere that prevailed in the campaign office. The organization had gone almost from one extreme to another.

When the campaign was over and PFC had won two of the three sought-after seats, it had to accomplish several tasks simultaneously: putting in place a mechanism to work with the two council members, developing its own structure, and furthering its political goal of electing progressives to local offices. These tasks revealed several other problematic issues.

The Purpose of the Coalition and Types of Participation.   After the election, the previously loosely organized coalition constituted a steering committee with representatives from participating organizations and unions who had been active in the coalition, and from geographical areas in the city corresponding to state House of Representatives districts. This structure helped to formalize and define the organization. Moreover, since the three neighborhood organizations could not formally participate, the geographical representatives could bring to PFC some of the localized issues that the neighborhood groups were pursuing. Steering committee meetings were open to anyone, but only formally elected or designated representatives could vote.

When the group coalesced in 1987, even though it decided to go forward with a third-party effort for the council seats, there was also sentiment to work within the Democratic party to attempt to change the nature of the Democratic Town Committee and create opportunities for more progressive candidates to win endorsement for slots on Democratic tickets. The PFC leadership attempted to define an organizational path of development that involved three aspects of work for the group: as a coalition, as a third party, and as activists within the Democratic party. The balance among these three roles was delicate and lent itself to several interpretations.

Some elements saw the PFC effort mainly as a means of changing the balance of forces within the Democratic party, particularly through changing the Town Committee, and viewed the third-party route as a more temporary tactic. For example, Phil Wheeler, the UAW participant (now the regional director for Region 9A) saw this direction of work as extremely important and thought that the third-party effort should eventually assume less importance. Since his union devoted a great deal of its political action apparatus to Democratic party work and the UAW leadership was quite committed to maintaining a role in the Democratic party, the third-party option was less important. Once PFC activists, constituting themselves as Democrats for Change, ran a slate in a Town Committee district, won the district, and went on to play a key role in unseating the incumbent Town Committee chairperson, the UAW had a sense of "mission accomplished" and was less concerned with the development of a strong third-party apparatus.

Other participants in PFC placed more emphasis on developing a permanent, left-progressive third party, both because they felt the need for such a political party and because they wanted to establish a more permanent force that would redefine debate within Hartford and pull the city's Democrats to the left. People with this view included several labor activists, several Puerto Rican Political Action Committee members, and other more leftward-oriented community activists.

District 1199's continued participation presented different issues. Their president envisioned the union's participation chiefly in elections, not as a permanent coalition member. Staff members and a number of rank-and-file members were very active as volunteers in the campaign. The 1199 office was used as election-day headquarters of the group, and many subsequent meetings took place there. But unless there was rank-and-file support for formally signing on, 1199'ers who participated would do so as individuals, not on behalf of the union. A formal resolution on the part of the union's executive board to participate as a member organization was never voted upon. District 1199 President Jerome (Jerry) Brown believes that elections rather than coalitions generate more enthusiasm among members, and that 1199's interests are more directly served through active participation in LEAP, due to the statewide focus more consistent with 1199's organizational structure. The specific local politics of Hartford are generally less important to the specific needs of the union.

Other union activists participate in PFC as representatives of unions that have varying degrees of interest in the affairs of PFC. The neighborhood organizations, as detailed above, do not formally participate; in time many of the activists from their ranks became less active and even hostile to the group. While the PFC council members attempted to represent the interests of the neighborhoods, PFC-sponsored initiatives at the council did not rally the neighborhood groups. Moreover, participation by people of color in PFC has been sporadic. These developments redefined PFC. The different degrees of participation on the part of organizations who were initially involved and the new issues that commanded PFC's attention geared it toward continually reasserting its political presence and contending with its minority-party status. For some organizations with pressing agendas of their own, PFC became less of a priority. Subsequent elections, which will not be analyzed here, even further redefined the political organization, although the 1991 election did give it more participation in City Hall.

OUTCOMES OF COALITION EFFORTS

The CLA, PFC and several other coalitions described at the beginning of this chapter are redefining issues, creating new demands on local government, and certainly redefining politics in Hartford. The

Colt situation provides one example. Without the CLA, much of the support for the strikers would not have been cultivated. Moreover, the strike experience contributed to the formation of People for Change.

Despite all of the problems analyzed earlier, the UAW leadership and strikers were extremely gratified with the degree of support for the strike achieved by the CLA's work. Hundreds of thousands of dollars were raised for the strikers' hardship funds. Political leaders were forced to take positions on the strike. Dozens of rallies involving literally thousands of people, mass pickets, and a civil disobedience action of forty-five union, political, community, and religious leaders—the "Colt 45"—kept the strike in the public eye. Police brutality on the picket line in the early months of the strike prompted marches to City Hall. While during the latter part of the fifty-month-long strike there was less activity than in the first year, CLA continued to meet several times a month. Once the union and other investors participated in a purchase of the company and the strike ended, the UAW and other organizations continued to meet and support other strikes in the area.

Redefinition of Public Issues

Besides providing material and moral support for the strikers, one of the major functions of the CLA was to place the issue in the public arena by calling for different forms of government intervention and for various organizations to take public actions and stances to support the strike. After the AFL-CIO launched a national boycott of Colt Firearms products, several state and local governments passed resolutions pledging not to buy any Colt Firearms products until the strike was settled. In Connecticut, the state legislature passed a resolution on the second anniversary of the strike calling for a negotiated settlement and curtailment of military contracts for Colt until a settlement was reached. The debate in the state capitol focused on whether the state should intervene or take a position in a "private" labor dispute. The campaign to halt

Pentagon contracts for the M16 rifle with Colt gained support in different parts of the country, and the union maintains that this campaign indeed caused Colt to lose its lucrative M16 contract and ultimately put the Firearms Division up for sale.

Shifting the issue of the strike into the public arena for public action also poised the UAW to become instrumental in launching PFC. The UAW leadership expected support from the Democratic party both in Hartford and statewide in its battle with Colt. Particularly when the Democratically controlled city government in Hartford did not fully embrace the strike as a critical issue and did not take decisive or supportive actions in such areas as complaints of police abuse, the UAW leadership became eager to take on those politicians. In concert with other groups who had strong grievances with local Democratic officeholders, the UAW's concerns would become part of a new political agenda that placed issues previously deemed private into the public domain.

This redefinition of issues for public attention is one consequence of organizations' responses to economic restructuring. And the process of redefinition itself generates controversy, as experienced in the debate within the Connecticut state legislature. However, many politicians embrace such issues as the Colt strike as important to the general welfare. The civil disobedience action, the "Colt 45" sit-in in May 1986, included three Democratic state representatives and a Republican city councilwoman. One of the three state representatives was Carrie Saxon Perry, who, as noted earlier, later became mayor of Hartford and continued to attend strike support functions, adding her name to various appeals on behalf of the strikers. During her first term as mayor, another lengthy strike began by the professional jai alai players in Hartford and at fourteen other frontons across the country (two others in Connecticut, one in Rhode Island, and eleven in Florida). Mayor Perry responded to the situation by meeting with the players and their families early in the strike and offering assistance. She was involved in rallies, meetings with other government officials, and other activities on behalf of the jai alai strikers. She routinely came to

1199's assistance in strikes at nursing homes, hospitals, and mental health facilities, and on other issues.

The Linkage Coalition, whose work culminated in 1986 with the defeat of ordinances that would have established a linkage policy in Hartford, also served to redefine the public agenda, and like the inaction in the Colt situation, anger over that defeat fueled the People for Change effort. The primary demand of the Linkage Coalition—an exaction fee on downtown development that would be used to create affordable housing and provide job training— generated resistance along the same lines as that generated by the Colt resolution in the General Assembly, that is, that intervention in the private market was not an appropriate role for government and would create a bad business climate. The Linkage Coalition, the CLA, PFC, and other coalitions, all attempt to redefine the public agenda and hence, redefine appropriate government action and intervention in this context of restructuring.

Creation of Demands on Local Government

Besides attempting to redefine what is an appropriate political agenda, organizations like the CLA, PFC, and other coalitions aggregate and articulate the claims of groups and individuals affected by economic restructuring by calling on municipal and state governments to mitigate the negative effects of economic restructuring. Local government in particular may seem more accessible to individuals than other levels of government, even though it has the least power to intervene in the economy and change or mediate national economic trends. However, residents of a city often know the individuals who sit on the city council and the small number of city council people in Hartford provides a very personal and familiar environment for local politics. Within this familiar environment, local residents attempt to exert demands on the government. Coalitions and neighborhood groups offer struc- tures for the presentation of such demands.

Several specific examples of the creation of new demands on

municipal government are illustrated by PFC's early work at the city council. Every year the council acts on a budget for the city. The council deliberations take place within party caucuses. Not surprisingly, throughout the 1980s the decisions of the Democratic Caucus were generally adopted, since their six-vote bloc prevailed. Whatever debates go on among Democrats are within the private caucus and they emerge as a united front.

During PFC's first city budget experience in 1988 the two council members and PFC activists fashioned a series of proposals to modify the budget in ways that would not cut essential services or cause municipal layoffs and would approximate a balanced budget. In that first budget cycle for PFC, the city faced the problems of declining state and federal aid, rising costs, and the possibility of either raising property taxes in order to pass a balanced budget or cutting the city manager's budget proposal to balance the budget. In 1988, PFC presented alternatives that its leadership knew might not necessarily receive serious attention by the Democrats, but could constitute a sound set of alternatives. Several measures they suggested were not passed during the budget process but were later adopted, since the city manager at the time and other Democratic council members found them to be attractive and sensible. One such proposal was the creation of an "infrastructure disruption fee" to be assessed upon firms whose construction projects disrupt traffic and other city functions.

In 1989, PFC decided to take a different approach to the budget process. Realizing that many hours had been expended in the 1988 process with no immediate returns, PFC activists launched a campaign known as the Neighborhood Power Campaign several months prior to the budget process; this campaign was designed to culminate in an alternative budget proposal. This budget alternative would not be based on line-by-line review, but upon a set of political priorities articulated through a series of community meetings under the auspices of the Neighborhood Power Campaign. Specific proposals would be based broadly on different forms of the linkage concept, all aimed at exacting new taxes and fees from corporations and developers.

These proposals were presented and discussed at the community meetings. Even if the proposals were not passed by the council, they could provide the basis for the 1989 campaign. Within the package of twenty-four budget resolutions were five that dealt specifically with concerns of labor; four of these revolved around issues that had surfaced in the Colt strike and the jai alai strike. The five resolutions included:

- a resolution to bill Colt Firearms and the jai alai fronton owner for the cost of police services at the picket line;
- a resolution to bill any firm involved in a strike 75 percent of the cost of police services at the strike;
- a resolution to recoup the costs of police services at the Colt strike from Colt Industries upon the sale of the company;
- a resolution requiring replacement workers in strikes to obtain licenses from the city at a cost of ninety-nine dollars, renewable annually;
- a resolution establishing a code of conduct for firms who enter agreements with the city for development and commerce mandating the firms' neutrality in union organizing drives.

None of these resolutions was passed, despite the fact that the same council previously passed several resolutions billing Colt for the cost of police services, resolutions Colt ignored. Many of the council Democrats had enjoyed labor's support and endorsements in prior campaigns.

These defeated resolutions were PFC's attempts to inject issues into municipal government policy that would defend the labor movement. The resolutions embodied approaches to the problem of union busting as it manifested inself in Hartford during the Colt strike. During their first term, PFC council members also introduced other resolutions of interest to labor without success. People for Change used this record during the 1989 campaign to generate support within the labor movement and was successful in obtaining endorsements and volunteers from a number of unions, some of whom had not been involved in PFC's 1987 campaign. These new claims on city government arise from the conditions in which labor finds itself as a result of economic restructuring, conditions that concern PFC activists.

Emergent Forms of Political Alignment

People for Change can be seen as a direct result of the political inaction on the part of local Democrats in areas that deeply concern and affect local people both in the workplace and in their neighborhoods. It is an attempt, however difficult and however immediately ineffectual, to create a new alignment in local politics in Hartford.

In one sense PFC's greatest accomplishment is that it has forced the Democratic party in the city to refocus direction. PFC is responsible for shifting the debate in the city council and in city politics more generally—providing an opening for new forms of political participation on the part of the city's large Puerto Rican population and crucial resources in the election of a progressive Puerto Rican state legislator. It has provided a vehicle for incorporation of specific demands of labor and the demands of the gay rights movement, and it is attempting to develop new African American political leaders. Despite its lack of success in winning votes at the city council in the first years of its existence, the climate of politics in Hartford has been changed considerably by its presence. During the 1991–1993 council term, many of PFC's proposals were taken with greater seriousness as it commanded a greater presence in the city, and after the November 1993 defeat, it announced its intention to maintain a political presence in Hartford.

Another important example of changing political alignments in this socioeconomic environment is that of LEAP. Although it operates on a statewide basis in Connecticut, LEAP also has considerable impact in Hartford. A number of large and influential unions participate in LEAP as a means of furthering their political goals, and in the course of their participation, they are drawn into issues beyond the usual agenda of labor. These unions also have a presence in Hartford, and many of them are involved in PFC. LEAP's assistance to PFC in the 1987 campaign was essential to the successful election of two PFC candidates.

As with PFC, the reaction to LEAP on the part of the more traditional Democrats is a measure of its success. LEAP earned the enmity of the state's governor, William O'Neill, through its association with O'Neill's Democratic challengers in past gubernatorial races. It has provided a highly competent, independent base of resources and personnel for many of the most progressive Democrats in the state legislature and has forced the Democratic party statewide to accommodate a large progressive bloc. LEAP-backed legislators helped to pass the Colt resolution in 1987 at the legislature. They waged an extremely complex and difficult battle in the 1989 session to avoid massive cuts in state services in spite of a serious budget crisis and, in 1991, succeeded in working with third-party governor Lowell Weicker to enact a state income tax. Through the UAW, the LEAP model is being "exported" to other states in New England and beyond.

Besides animosity and suspicion from the mainstream Democratic party machine, LEAP also became a source of controversy within the top leadership levels of the AFL-CIO. Elements of the Connecticut AFL-CIO who were tied into the state Democratic party attempted to bring pressure from national AFL-CIO leadership to bar the participation of local labor councils in LEAP. They attempted to portray LEAP as under "Communist influence," a stale McCarthyite tactic that was unconvincing. When local labor council presidents refused to succumb to the AFL-CIO's pressure, the national leadership abandoned their attempts to bar participation in such organizations (Brecher and Costello 1990).

CONCLUSIONS

Coalition work is producing results and achieving new significance to the organizations in this book. Yet the importance attributed to this work varies greatly from organization to organization. For the unions, the concept of labor solidarity provides an opening for coalition participation, despite suspicion from conservative state and national leadership elements about specific coalition formations. But among the neighborhood groups, the inherent turf orientation and the human resource demands of other issues seem to contribute to an inability to fully embrace coalitions, even though some staff members realize their value.

Perhaps the process of working together, either casually and occasionally or more intensely, helps to break down barriers. Awareness of each other's respective organizational agendas and priorities helps to create new ways of thinking and behaving. Specifically, in the summer of 1989, HART members became concerned about developers' buying parcels of land in quiet residential blocks and erecting large multiunit condominiums. They issued a call for a moratorium on all development in several specific residential zones for 120 days to allow the city government time to conduct impact studies and HART more time to respond to this issue. In the past in Hartford, opposition to such a call could be expected from the Building Trade Unions (a significant bloc within the Greater Hartford Labor Council), who previously opposed similar neighborhood organizations' demands. In this instance, however, the president of the labor council, who had been meeting monthly with neighborhood organizations for close to two years in the Grassroots-Labor Forum described above, came to a HART meeting on June 7, 1989, to say that since the proposed moratorium did not impact construction projects that employed union labor, the central labor council would remain neutral on the issue and not lobby in opposition to such a construction moratorium. The significance of this action was probably lost on most of the HART members in attendance, but it represented a relatively new type of relationship between labor and community forces.

Recognition of the validity of the neighborhood organization's agenda in this instance meant that elements in the local labor council felt it was important to support rather than alienate a neighborhood organization such as HART. They were beginning to see beyond the narrow interpretation of self-interest that is often attributed to labor.

An important difference between the two types of organizations is in the nature of the targets of the respective organizational campaigns. Both labor and neighborhood organizations may work against corporate interests, but these corporate interests are involved in different sectors of the economy. Sometimes their targets may overlap—a downtown development project involving a new hotel may bring together neighborhood organizations demanding jobs during construction and in the finished project with a labor union such as HERE that would be interested in organizing the workers in the completed hotel, as happened in New Haven, Connecticut. Often the threat of plant closings in a community can bring labor and neighborhood forces together, but such a scenario has not developed in Hartford. Until the targets of a particular union and a particular neighborhood group overlap exactly, the opportunities presented by their respective methods of organizing will not likely be fully understood or utilized.

The experiences described in this chapter demonstrate how some of the rationales behind neighborhood organizing and labor organizing confront each other in coalition activities. Different logics are employed, and strategies and tactics are built upon different premises. However, as distinct as the organizations are, the differences are not insurmountable if both sides want to work in coalitions and can engage in the art of compromise. Much depends upon how any single organization assesses its individual capacity to achieve a particular goal—if it knows it cannot "go it alone," then it attempts to work through coalitions.

Coalitions, specifically electoral coalitions, can become mired in the "trenches" of urban problems as Katznelson (1981) illustrates—infighting, ethnic and racial rivalries, and turf-oriented sparring. PFC has to function in a political environment fraught with such pitfalls, yet LEAP has a very successful record of defining an agenda and not succumbing to a great deal of interorganizational disputes. It will only take on major projects agreeable to all participants and work on commonly defined and agreed-upon goals.

The UAW and 1199 have very direct involvement in electoral politics and participate in myriad political activities, while HERE has significantly less participation. When the governor is the "boss," as is the case with 1199, the union must engage in an interesting balancing act counterposing the need for access to political officials through both formal and informal means with the need to be taken seriously by the same officials and demonstrate strength through militant tactics. Political involvement, therefore, is considered very important by District 1199 union leadership. The UAW's inherited tradition of political involvement and the individual involvement of its leaders in the Democratic party lead that union into many forms of political action.

These partisan political involvements highlight the deepest distinctions between the neighborhood organizations and the unions. The union with the most experience in coalitions with the neighborhood organizations, the UAW, has the greatest difficulty countenancing this distinction and cannot understand the lack of desire for partisan political involvement by neighborhood group leadership. The neighborhood organizations have very little recourse at this stage in their development to pursue political action even if their leadership so wishes, although as has been noted, they do command a quasi-political presence in Hartford. This gulf is a serious barrier to more permanent alliances between the two types of organizations.

THREE

Labor Organizing

The Colt strike was a focal point for the labor movement in Hartford in the 1980s. As a major victory for the labor movement and its community allies, it became an example of the meaning unions still have and the sacrifices individuals are still willing to endure. Its importance lies both in the traditional strike drama between unions and management at the factory gate and in the strategies developed to meet a new climate of labor relations. Within this climate, organizing new members, developing existing membership to meet their challenges, and simply keeping a union organization together are all immensely difficult.

ORGANIZING NEW MEMBERS

The organizing of new members is being both refined and redefined in the environment of economic restructuring. Several aspects of union organizing in the Hartford area illustrate these adaptations: who is being organized and how, including the use of new organizing models; the organizing campaign process itself and the thorny issue of recognition strikes; and, moreover, the place of organizing within the overall framework of the union.

The Pool of New Members

One aspect of organizing new members relates to who is being organized. For the UAW, organizing is wide open in the Hartford area in terms of the industries and types of workers approached.

Historically the UAW has organized manufacturing concerns in the area—precisely the industries who have moved operations out of the region. In fact, the UAW leadership estimates that the union lost at least half of its membership in the region between 1970 and the late 1980s. Currently, the UAW organizes in virtually any industry from which interested workers approach the union. Within the New England states' Region 9A, recently organized workers include public employees on Cape Cod, maintenance workers at the University of Hartford, and cafeteria workers in the East Lyme, Connecticut, school system, who are employed by the Marriott Corporation. This contrasts with HERE and 1199, both of which continue to organize generally within the industries indicated by their respective names: hotels and restaurants, including cafeteria workers in public institutions and colleges; and the entire health care industry, from mental health and retardation group homes to public employees in the health fields.

New organizing is taking place within the context of simultaneous erosion of existing membership bases for many unions. While the UAW feels the impact of economic restructuring through the restructuring of manufacturing, the other unions are not immune to analogous problems in their industries. HERE must face the reality of restaurant and hotel closures and downsizing. During the time in which this research was under way, two of Hartford's major hotels closed, the Hartford Hilton and the Summit Hotel, and HERE lost three hundred members. District 1199 had to deal with the affiliation of Hartford's fiscally troubled Mt. Sinai Hospital, in which several departments are organized by 1199, with St. Francis Hospital, a totally nonunion hospital. All of these unions are affected by different forms of restructuring, and their organizing strategies must accommodate this reality.

New Organizing Models: The Blitz

While one of the major methods by which the UAW has adapted to changing conditions has been to organize new sectors, HERE and 1199 have adapted by maximizing the organizing they do undertake, which involves moving in and out of organizing situations rapidly and concentrating on drives where success seems more likely. HERE and 1199 have adopted models referred to as the 1-2-3 method and the Blitz, respectively, in which at several key points early in the drive, the unions assess their strength and decide either to continue or to halt the drive. Both make extensive use of home visits and one-to-one meetings with workers in environments where they feel comfortable discussing their concerns. The UAW also uses similar methods in some of the organizing drives it undertakes.

The Blitz model developed by 1199 has been used successfully in organizing nursing homes of approximately 120 workers in urban areas; it has also been applied to community-based mental health facilities in Connecticut. HERE's similar 1–2–3 model is used in small to medium-sized hotels, although the pacing is sometimes slower than that of the Blitz. These models were developed in response to the increasingly sophisticated and virulent antiunion campaigns of employers and the delays encountered during the course of organizing drives as employers stall the process at the National Labor Relations Board (NLRB). The Blitz attempts to maximize union contact with the workers before the employer discovers that the union has been approached and essentially compresses the time frame of the initial stages of organizing drives as compared to drives that were conducted ten to fifteen years ago. It involves several key factors early in the campaign: leadership, speed, and motivation.

The essential elements of the model are as follows. In less than a week after the union is first contacted by workers interested in organizing, the union organizers attempt to meet with workers— generally through home visits—who are identified by other workers as leaders. The organizers hold initial meetings to ascertain the degree of interest among these leaders in establishing an organizing committee; they then hold an organizing committee meeting, after which they assess the potential for a successful campaign. This assessment is based on the anticipated response and resources available to the employer to fight the union, as well as on the capacity of the workers to organize.

Leaders are defined very simply: people whom other people follow. The leadership quality can be strictly social and unrelated to particular work site issues or it can be tied specifically to the workplace. The key criterion is that a leader have influence over others. Organizers estimate that there is roughly a one-to-five ratio of leaders to the rest of the workers at a given work site.

Speed, specifically in reaching leaders, is very important in the early stages of a campaign: The union wants to reach the maximum number of people before the employer catches on. The goal is to identify leaders in the first three days and have time with these leaders to "inoculate" them against employer propaganda and antiunion arguments. Organizers realize that during this first week of the campaign the employer will undoubtedly find out that the union has been contacted, but they try to maintain a degree of secrecy and keep control of information and the pacing of organizing within the union's province as long as possible. Employers often try to dissuade leaders from continuing their participation in the drive or else work to erode support among nonleaders, whichever method most effectively stymies unionization.

Worker motivation is another consideration: The union does not want to invest limited resources in losing campaigns, and therefore the determination must be made quickly as to whether sufficient motivation exists among the workers to sustain and win a campaign. The organizers base the assessment on a number of questions: Is there sufficient anger toward the employer and intensity about the desire to organize? Do leaders feel this anger personally, not necessarily "for" others, but for themselves? Is there unity or division among the workers? Will the leaders accept responsibility and take on tasks to move the effort forward?

Workers' willingness to take assignments is critically important in an organizer's assessment and is a key factor in determining whether to continue the campaign. The tasks and responsibilities that workers are asked to assume involve risk and test commitment, and yet organizers are trained not to ask workers prematurely to do risky things that could frighten them away from the campaign. For example, workers may be asked to set up meetings with coworkers, to begin to persuade coworkers as to the benefits of organizing, to devise lists of coworkers' names, addresses, and telephone numbers, or other tasks necessary to the campaign.

The first concrete test of the workers, particularly the leaders, is the attendance at the initial organizing committee meeting: Are leaders there and have they brought others? Is approximately 70 percent of the work force represented? If there is insufficient attendance or representation from different work areas, the union may at that point pull out of the effort with the understanding that if events in the future generate a higher level of interest in organizing, the workers should again contact the union. In these instances an organizer may remain in communication with some of the key activists from the workplace. If the campaign does proceed after key point, it generally moves all the way to a collective-bargaining election, although occasionally the union will pull out just before an election if the prognosis is particularly grim.

If there is sufficient attendance and motivation evidenced at the first committee meeting, then a "card rally" is set for a few days later. At this rally (which is actually an expanded and more spirited committee meeting), organizers play a key role: answering questions, developing a sense of unity among the various groups of workers, detailing what employer reaction is likely to be—the antiunion tactics that workers can anticipate—and passing out union cards. In these meetings organizers caution that it may be necessary to strike to gain union recognition. They are frank about the potential hardships ahead in the campaign, but they also show what workers stand to gain. Workers from unionized institutions may speak at the meetings and attest to the kinds of changes in the work environment that unionization makes possible.

The workers then have approximately seventy-two hours to distribute and retrieve signed union cards authorizing the union to represent the signer. Once these cards are back to the organizer, and if at least 70 percent of the work force has signed, some type of demonstrative action takes place in front of the employer demanding union recognition. In the vast majority of cases, the employer refuses recognition based on a show of union authorization cards and the union then petitions the NLRB for a collective-bargaining election.

After the Blitz: Aspects of the Remainder
of the Campaign

Although most organizing drives eventually end up in NLRB-sponsored elections, the union resists ceding control of the time frame and scheduling to an outside entity for as long as possible. Once the NLRB is petitioned, the process of determining unit size must take place, and the employer has available, and often uses, many opportunities to stall the campaign. At this point the blitz aspect of the organizing drive is over. A hearing must be held to determine the unit size, and then an election date is set.

Unit size can be very important to the success of an organizing drive. During the 1980s, NLRB decisions about appropriate unit size for purposes of conducting elections stipulated larger units, including many different groups of workers, an arrangement that gives employers, and, in the case of 1199, specifically hospitals, an advantage. According to 1199 as many as eight groups of workers with distinct interests may exist at a typical hospital and determinations about the size of units should reflect these divisions rather than the preference of hospital managements for larger units. After these rulings, 1199 and other unions attempting to organize hospitals had very few successes, and 1199 began to focus its organizing energies on smaller health care institutions such as nursing homes and group homes. The union's chances for success are much greater when organizing smaller, more cohesive groups of workers.

Generally the election takes place at least a month later if there is minimal disagreement between the employer and union in determining the unit. If there is disagreement, several appearances before the NLRB may be required, and the process can drag on while enthusiasm for the union among the workers can die. The union at this point may attempt to circumvent the process by threatening to strike even before an election is set if the employer's tactics are terribly obstructionist. Even if the situation does not deteriorate to that extent, the union's major task, specifically the job of the organizer, from this point on is to maintain enthusiasm and support for the union among the workers. This is also the point where the role of consultants or attorneys engaging in the modern union-busting strategies promulgated during recent decades may become more prominent.

During this crucial period between filing a petition at the NLRB and the election, the degree of responsibility assumed by the organizing committee is most critical. Training for organizers emphasizes that the organizer must not take on all of the responsibility in the campaign, that is, take on the role of the "best organizing committee member," but rather delegate tasks so that workers essentially organize themselves with guidance from the organizer. In turn, organizers spend time training the organizing committee on how to keep the campaign moving forward and what to expect from the employer.

The employer's response to the unionization attempt always has the potential to create fear among the workers—the fear of losing one's livelihood—not at all unfounded (see Goldfield 1987). This preelection period is a likely time for workers to be fired or harassed and also for union-busting consultants to be retained by employers. A wide range of employer tactics may be confronted in organizing drives. One tactic used by union-busting consultants is to fire supervisors, either to instill fear in the entire work force or to appease workers who dislike a particular supervisor. Sometimes consultants develop and use psychological profiles of workers during antiunion campaigns. Workers in smaller workplaces seem to be best able to withstand the antiunion activities. However, certain consultants boast extremely effective records specifically against 1199.

District 1199 in turn trains and prepares workers in organizing drives for the employer's response. One typical employer tactic portrays the union as an outside third party that will complicate future relationships between the workers and the employer. Another is to admit that some things have been done incorrectly in the past and to ask for another chance. The cost of union dues is emphasized, often with graphic illustrations such as the amount of groceries equivalent to a year's union dues. Divisions among the workers along racial and ethnic lines may be exploited or fostered. Movies about past 1199 strikes are often shown with the intention of portraying 1199 as a violent union. If the work force is predominantly Black, the union is characterized as a Jewish Communist union. If the work force is predominantly white, the union is characterized as a Black militant union. (In the case of HERE, employers have characterized the union as mob-controlled.) One of the union's responses is to develop outside support from respected political, religious, and community leaders—often the Black clergy. However, 1199 has faced situations in southern states where employers countered by retaining a group of Black ministers from different southern cities who traveled to work sites where union drives were under way and preached antiunion messages.

In past years, many of these activities took place at "captive audience" meetings during the workday, sometimes leaving patients unattended. However, employers are now emphasizing "one-on-one" (or two- or three-on-one) encounters: meetings with individual workers in which two or more supervisors interrogate or scream at the worker, usually within eyesight or earshot of other workers. It is often in this atmosphere that workers have to decide whether they want a union.

While the organizer is employed full-time to do his or her job and is involved in campaign after campaign, the workers at an individual workplace are attempting to unionize more often than not for the first time, in response to the individual employer or supervisor or working conditions. As Piven and Cloward (1977) point out, workers do not experience "class struggle," they experience the unfairness of a particular employer. They call the union because of their specific circumstances. The organizer, by way of warning the workers about all of the various devices used by employers, shows the workers how their specific circumstances fit into the overall pattern of labor relations. So while the employer is characterized and responded to on the basis of individual behavior, he or she is also characterized in more generic terms as a "boss," behaving as bosses behave. The organizers consciously convey a picture of adversarial class relations in society and believe that this is important in the course of organizing in order to motivate and strengthen the workers' resolve.

The Recognition Strike

Another feature of contemporary organizing involves the recognition strike. While every aspect of labor relations has become exceedingly difficult in the past decade, obtaining a first contract after a successful organizing drive is one of the most formidable tasks facing unions. Whereas the distinction between an unfair labor practice strike and an economic strike is essentially based on legal status with legal implications, the recognition strike can be either: It may or may not involve unfair labor practices, but it usually takes place as the result of failed negotiations for a first contract after workers vote for unionization in an NLRB-supervised election. In rare instances, the union may call a strike when the employer refuses to agree to an election.

If the union can document unfair labor practices in the course of the negotiations for the first contract and then strikes, it can file charges with the NLRB asking the Board to charge the company with unfair labor practices. If, after a trial, these charges are sustained by an administrative law judge, the judge may order the reinstatement of the workers. However, a recognition strike without allegations of unfair labor practices is an immense gamble: Once the workers walk out the employer's door, they may be out forever if permanent replacement workers are hired. Even those unions who eschew heavy reliance on legal strategies pursue this route to hedge against the very real threat of permanent replacements.

All three of the unions in this research have at various times found themselves in strikes over union recognition and in most instances have attempted to transform the strike into an unfair labor practices strike. During this process union members and any outside supporters tend not to use the term "recognition strike" either in public—to emphasize that the employer broke the law and to strengthen the case before the NLRB—or in private—to boost the morale of strikers who may be reassured by the legal protection implied in the term "unfair labor practices" strike.

One example of this strategy was the strike by professional jai alai players that began in April 1988. The International Jai Alai Players Association (IJAPA) declared a strike in order to gain union recognition and, soon after beginning the strike, approached the UAW for affiliation. Three jai alai frontons operate in Connecticut (others are in Rhode Island and Florida), and the IJAPA leadership was based at the Hartford fronton. The UAW Region 9A leadership was willing to take risks with this group of strikers who were inexperienced in the intricacies of labor relations, and shepherded the process of affiliation through the UAW hierarchy. If the players were successful in their attempt to unionize, once the strike was finished the UAW would gain several hundred new members in an industry new to the UAW, professional sports. When IJAPA formally became affiliated with the UAW, the regional leadership began to shape the strike strategy into an unfair-labor-practices strategy. Accordingly strikers and supporters ceased referring to the strike as a recognition strike.

The Culture of Organizing

Perhaps one of the most important variables involved in organizing the unorganized is the degree of importance attached to this work by the union and how the union's philosophy incorporates new organizing. David Pickus, the 1199–New England vice-president for organizing, refers to this as the "culture of organizing." 1199 has historically devoted a great deal of resources to organizing new groups of workers and frames the issue of organizing not simply in terms of obtaining larger membership rolls for the union itself, but also in terms of empowering the working class in general, and health care workers in particular (see Fink and Greenberg 1989). 1199's New England staff is designed to accommodate this mission through its officer structure, which includes a vice-president for organizing, and its staffing pattern, which includes an organizing team of at least three "field organizers," those staff members assigned to organize the unorganized. Field organizers may also be asked to participate in organizing drives of national importance to the union and assume temporary assignments on the West Coast, in the South, or elsewhere.

HERE Local 217 likewise places a heavy emphasis on organizing new members and has reorganized its staff in recent years to enhance its organizing capacity. The emphasis on organizing by HERE has yielded some notable successes in the area: HERE Local 217 was the key force for organizing Yale employees in New Haven who, once organized, chartered new locals with the international union.

The UAW in this region has five staff members assigned to new organizing, and locals may also undertake organizing drives. New organizing is assuming a more prominent role for the UAW, and, as noted in the beginning of this chapter, this is among groups of workers not previously considered UAW targets for organizing.

Probably more than anything else, organizing the unorganized in this era requires an ability to constantly refine and reassess techniques and strategies. 1199 organizers—many only in their thirties and forties—reminisce about organizing techniques of as recently as fifteen years ago, when the organizer would begin a drive by distributing leaflets to workers at shift changes in front of a facility. Any interested workers would be asked to join an organizing committee, authorization cards would be handed out continuously, and once approximately 65 to 75 percent of the work force had signed cards, the workers and the organizer would march on the boss and demand recognition. All of this was much more public and much less precise than contemporary practices. Organizing was not easy then, but it is excruciating today, given managements' new techniques, the manner in which labor law is currently interpreted and enforced, and the difficult climate for unions generally. Therefore, the importance attached to organizing the unorganized and the tenacity of the union leadership in maintaining the "culture of organizing" in the midst of the drastic changes in the organizing environment are critical to sustaining and enhancing the union's capacity for growth and empowerment.

MEMBERSHIP MOBILIZATION

At a time when unions are besieged by the external challenges discussed earlier, the requirements and demands involved in satisfying membership needs are innumerably varied and complex. Indeed for each employer, for each industry, for each sector of the economy, strategies and tactics must be devised and constantly reformulated as even newer problems present themselves. Certain types of problems pertain only to specific work sites, while others are more generalized problems of the current labor relations environment. In the several years that the three unions were observed, they collectively confronted quite a wide range of issues: industrial restructuring and contraction of firms' operations; foreign competition; mergers and acquisitions; managements set on breaking the union at specific work sites; plant closings; demands for concessions from employers; rising health care costs, from the standpoint of both health care consumers and workers in the health care industry; fiscal crises of both state and local governments; publicly regulated industries and the resulting bureaucratic entanglements; privatization of public services; economic swings in consumer leisure spending; regional and local economic development patterns and shifts; local, regional, and national political climates; cumbersome legal processes in the NLRB bureaucracy; divergent philosophies and ideologies within the trade union movement; lack of understanding within the larger community of the role and mission of organized labor; and the relative ease of replacing union workers with nonunion workers during strikes.

And there are more. All of these issues require analysis, action, and varying degrees of membership involvement and mobilization if there is to be any hope of successful resolution for the members' benefit. The unions' responses to this problematic environment illustrate the challenges: shop floor and work site issues and power relationships; union viewpoints as presented in organizational media and other internal educational activities and the impact of these messages; and external relationships with other unions and in political processes and strike strategies. While several of these areas arose in the discussion of coalitions, here they are considered in terms of how unions themselves function, make choices, and take action.

Shop Floor and Work Site Issues

All three unions must develop among their rank-and-file members the capacity to deal with work site issues and confront employers, usually the first level of supervisors, every day without the assistance of union staff people or perhaps initially even a union steward. This is the most basic form of empowerment afforded through unionization. There is generally an apparatus of stewards (or "delegates" as 1199 refers to them) and some type of shop committee. This level of organization is truly the lifeblood of the union and makes the difference between a workplace in which workers feel a sense of, and can exercise, power and one in which worker apathy and disorganization reign.

Various training activities are undertaken by the unions to develop the leadership skills necessary to function on the shop floor level. All experiment with new activities and formats. One method used fairly regularly by the unions is a workshop setting with simulations and role-playing. Workers are given a hypothetical problem to react to, and they assume different roles in the situation: typically the boss, the worker(s), and the steward. This format not only yields knowledge about specific techniques but often helps foster a sense of camaraderie among the workers—another very necessary component of successful shop committees.

HERE 217 training emphasizes first and foremost the issue of developing a "fight," that is, "getting the victim to fight" and "pushing people to win, not whine." The steward does not do "for" others but builds the workers' collective ability to confront issues. Careful preparation and anticipation of the employer's reactions are emphasized. Fairness for the affected workers and future implications of any problem resolution are also stressed.

District 1199 frames the question of shop floor activity in terms of worker power and unity. It has developed a training module for organizers and rank-and-file leaders that is offered periodically to groups of organizers and active members from various sites. The objectives of the training are: (1) to teach that the source of workers' power is their united action; (2) to teach that an organizer's job is *not* to solve problems but to lead workers into struggle so they learn from their experience that their power comes from their united action; and (3) to introduce principles and concepts to help leaders think, plan, and function as organizers.

An important theme that applies to 1199's approach to the entire range of union issues is that of the union's being an "instrument of workers' power" rather than a "service organization." This theme also helps to explain 1199's aversion to reliance on attorneys and legal procedures, and more generally, how it distinguishes itself from other unions who do envision their roles more as service organizations. The 1199 training activities are geared toward developing the capacity for militance and activism among organizers and members.

Although the unions want to train workers to handle problems and empower themselves, the leadership does not necessarily envision every issue as developing into a major confrontation. Union leaders are interested in instilling in the employer a "healthy respect" for the power of the unionized workers so that employers have to think of the implications of their decisions and actions as they affect the union members. This means that workers may have to exercise their power dramatically on a periodic basis, but not over every single issue. In other words, the union's potential to disrupt work site activity is an important means of exercising its power.

Shop floor leadership and organization is critically important during intense labor-management conflict. In the Colt Firearms situation, prior to the beginning of the strike in January 1986, the UAW members at Colt staged what they call an "in-plant strike" for nine months after the expiration of their previous contract in April 1985. During this time, a virtual underground existed in which the shop committee coordinated job actions and kept track of employer violations of labor law in an effort to build a case for later legal action. As antagonisms deepened between the workers and the management, simultaneously the anger and resolve that would propel and sustain the workers during the eventual four-year-long strike was also developing.

Developing Membership Power: Media, Messages, and Assemblies

A broad range of membership development activities are undertaken by the three unions. One important aspect of this process is the ideological message that the union leadership wants to impart to the members. Several methods are used to transmit organizational points of view: Conferences, conventions, and printed materials provide support for workers in their workplaces and communities as they confront issues and struggles.

Union conferences, conventions, and regular assemblies offer key opportunities to present organizational viewpoints. The messages conveyed at such events are especially important because among the three unions' memberships are many people with limited formal education, people who speak limited English or read virtually no English, as well as people who are not necessarily accustomed to a great deal of reading. Therefore, speeches or oral presentations at union activities may be a primary method of obtaining information for these members, and oral and slide or video presentations are effective methods for transmitting content and themes to many union members.

Presentations at 1199 conventions emphasize an analysis of shifts in the economy, the ideology and policy orientation of the national administrations, and the implications for workers, specifically health care workers, with the conclusion that unionization is the most important vehicle to address the problems. Despite concerns about whether 1199 members who hear such presentations will fully comprehend them and remember their fine points, these are genuine attempts at distilling complicated material for average workers and arming them with sophisticated arguments. More fundamentally, these presentations represent the type of analysis that informs 1199's praxis and the message its leadership attempts to impart to members.

Within its meetings, conferences, and union literature, 1199 regularly invokes the memory and words of Dr. Martin Luther King, Jr., who participated in various 1199 campaigns during his life, and it also maintains a relationship with Coretta Scott King. Inasmuch as this union often characterizes its mission as an extension of the civil rights movement into the economic sphere, locally and nationally it has allied with various civil rights organizations, as well as with coalitions and organizations concerned with American foreign policy. An emphasis on activism and social justice pervades most of 1199's activities and publications, consistent with its left-wing heritage (see Fink and Greenberg 1989).

In recent years 1199 has cultivated a relationship with the Reverend Jesse Jackson and was one of the only national labor unions to endorse him in his 1988 presidential campaign. Many of the Jackson campaign themes have been incorporated into the 1199 repertoire. During Jackson's campaign stops in Hartford, 1199 leaders and staff were integrally involved in organizing and moderating rallies. In 1991, the union helped coordinate Jackson's "March to Rebuild America" through Connecticut.

Many of the HERE Local 217 organizers likewise are from activist backgrounds and view their work as extensions of social movements, including the civil rights and women's movements, as well as community organizing. Union issues are often presented to members as questions of power and the results of class or power relationships in the larger society. Efforts to ally their union issues with larger civil rights issues were evident in the 1988 Yale University labor negotiations. When the Yale locals were on the verge of a strike at the university in 1988, one of their strategies was to invite Jesse Jackson to speak at a large community support rally on the Yale campus. Jackson, of course, benefited from his appearance: Through this activity he was able to cultivate a relationship with an additional segment of the labor movement and secure the support of these unions in his presidential campaign. The relationship between civil rights and labor issues was also stressed during Local 217's 1987 strike at the Hartford Sheraton. Key support came from Hartford mayor Carrie Saxon Perry who, in speeches at various rallies, highlighted these relationships.

The perspectives of the UAW as outlined within its publications may be described as solidly within the liberal-left Democratic party realm, emphasizing an economic interventionist role for government and the need for such measures as an industrial policy. However, a more general theme of economic justice within the country is also emphasized, especially for minority and urban populations, as well as concern for workers' lives beyond the workplace and into political and community activities, even recreational or leisure endeavors.

The UAW regional organization is able to draw upon the resources of its parent international union in delivering an organizational point of view and also takes advantage of the international's facility in northern Michigan, the Walter and May Reuther Family Education Center at Black Lake. Every year UAW members from different locals within Region 9A take part in the educational programs offered at Black Lake, as well as educational programs offered through the Region 9A office. However, there are also the more informal ideological and educational avenues, including speakers at meetings and rallies, particularly in activities of the Community Action Program Council.

During the Colt strike, International UAW speakers who were featured at the major local rallies consistently emphasized the same progressive social democratic themes as in the union's various printed materials. As one would expect, the speakers decried the tedious NLRB processes and the greed of Colt and other union-busting employers; but they also recounted the need for national solutions to economic problems and the necessity for political involvement of the strikers and their allies.

The rhetoric of the UAW message is perhaps not as radical that as of 1199, but the message does draw on the industrial policy literature of the mid-1980s, which became familiar to graduate students in the political economy or industrial relations fields. Again, how much of the written material the average worker may comprehend is difficult to estimate, yet many Colt strikers who were active in union-sponsored events during the strike were fully capable of articulating the relationship between their experience and the national political-economic climate.

Estimating the Impact of Union Messages

The Colt strikers are a segment of UAW Region 9A's membership who relied heavily on the support and resources of the union structure beyond the local level from both the regional and international offices of the organization. The union was an important part of their lives, and, regardless of their level of union participation before the strike, as a group they developed an intense loyalty to the UAW. One might therefore expect that these strikers would share and adopt many of the themes prominent in UAW publications and articulated by UAW leadership. Proving such an assertion is difficult. However, some preliminary conclusions about the opinions of the strikers may be drawn from a research project undertaken by Marc Lendler in 1989 on the changing authority structures in the lives of the Colt strikers. Part of his research involved a survey administered to 253 strikers in the spring of 1989. The survey was administered randomly to strikers who attended one of the weekly membership meetings during April 1989. At these meetings, strikers received their $100-per-week strike benefits and were brought up to date on strike-related events.

The answers to several of Lendler's questions regarding political participation reveal a high percentage of respondents who voted in the 1988 presidential election, 87 percent, and of those who voted, 92.6 percent voted for Dukakis. In a statewide poll of Connecticut union members conducted by the University of Connecticut's Institute for Social Inquiry, 55 percent of respondents (N=106) voted for Dukakis. When asked to assess Reagan's presidency, 71.5 percent of the Colt striker survey respondents felt that he was a "poor" president, 22.2 percent felt he was "only fair," while only 5.0 percent felt he was a "good" president, and 1.3 percent felt he was "very good." Although these results are not surprising given the strikers' experiences, they do demonstrate a consistency with the themes emphasized by the UAW in its various media.

The survey results also suggested that involvement in the strike stimulated new and greater levels of political participation among some of the strikers. The combination of the union leadership's guidance and urging, coupled with the necessity of political involvement during the strike most likely produced these results. However, Lendler's survey provides some indication that the rank-and-file strikers' shared the union leadership's assessment of the situation.

Strategies, Mobilizations, and Interunion Relationships

The three unions employ a variety of strategies to achieve their goals, including rallies, marches, picketing, lobbying, civil disobedience, targeting of specific public officials, and other techniques. Many strategies are applied universally: All establish picket lines during strikes; all hold rallies and call upon other unions to attend and contribute financially to strike efforts; and all three interact with political officials on their respective issues. Yet in certain instances, these unions use rather bold tactics, both in terms of the risks union members are willing to take and the possible outcomes that might result from the actions. Several strategies are analyzed below in terms of both their rationales and their impact, as well as how these can be considered innovations in attempting to meet the unions' current challenges. Moreover, relationships with other unions also affect the ability to achieve their goals.

The Use of Protest and Routine Political Strategies.   In a number of situations, the unions used protest tactics in a manner corresponding to Lipsky's (1970) model of protest in which "reference publics"—those to whom the decision makers feel accountable and whose pressure might overtly or patently be brought to bear in the situation—are specified as protest targets. However, protest was also utilized as a means of exerting pressure on the targets directly. For example, in the spring of 1989, 1199 was involved in contract negotiations with the state of Connecticut for seven thousand state health care workers, a situation eventually resolved through binding arbitration. Leading up to that point, the union leadership wanted to facilitate membership participation and present a militant, determined stance to the state's negotiators. Accordingly, the union sponsored several demonstrations in the area around the state capitol building and state office buildings in Hartford. During these demonstrations, 1199 members blocked traffic and sat down in the middle of a busy intersection in front of the capitol and burned a copy of the state's last contract offer, which was being submitted to the arbitrator as the state's final position.

In these instances, the union was attempting several things simultaneously: maintaining the membership's vocal involvement and participation; and exerting pressure on the state bureaucracy without altogether alienating the governor, who might ultimately involve himself in the negotiations with favorable results for the union. This delicate balancing act finally resulted in an arbitration award that the union considered acceptable.

The UAW conducted several marches at the state capitol directed at the governor during the course of the Colt strike. One march called on him to use his office to bring the two parties together for negotiations. Governor O'Neill had intervened in other strikes, but generally this had occurred when the possibility for a settlement was at hand, for example, at an 1199 strike at Waterbury (Connecticut) Hospital in the fall of 1986. He apparently perceived no such possibility in the early months of the Colt strike and, moreover, had an antagonistic relationship with the UAW regional director at the time, John Flynn. Flynn was very active in Democratic party politics, but as a leader of the rival, more liberal faction associated with LEAP. The UAW leadership felt that O'Neill's lack of involvement until much later, when the company was being sold, stemmed from these political differences, and accordingly, O'Neill became an ancillary target during the strike.

In public statements, the UAW leadership constantly challenged O'Neill to help settle the strike. In 1989, another demonstration took place at the state capitol after the union discovered that the state of Connecticut continued to purchase weapons from Colt for its law enforcement personnel despite a national AFL-CIO-sponsored boycott of Colt Firearms and the Connecticut General Assembly resolution urging the Pentagon not to purchase Colt products until the strike was resolved. These demonstrations were readily attended by strikers, who had grown very critical of, and felt great animosity toward, O'Neill for perceived inaction on their behalf.

The UAW and 1199 enjoyed very different relationships with the governor during his term of office. A sit-in at the Department of Mental Retardation central office that resulted in arrests is one of many demonstrations 1199 held at state offices. O'Neill himself, however, was rarely the target of the demonstrations. Rather it was the legislature, commissioners of various state agencies, the budget office, among others—not the governor, personally. This enabled the governor to intervene and "fix" certain situations at the eleventh hour. For example, O'Neill's intervention just before threatened strikes at community mental health and mental retardation facilities that subcontracted from the state produced settlements instead of strikes in 1987 and 1990.

The 1199 leadership attributes O'Neill's cooperation to the fact that he took the union's threat to strike seriously and respected its power. If 1199 struck state agencies or subcontractors, it would wreak havoc for the state bureaucracy and could bring criticism to the state government leadership. However, in contrast, the UAW's relationship with O'Neill was not nearly as complex: Except for the jai alai players, UAW members did not work under O'Neill's direct or indirect chain of command, and therefore his action or inaction in the Colt strike remained confined to that one situation, without the lasting implications that his actions with 1199 might signify.

While HERE 217 has few occasions to make the state government or the governor a direct target in their various struggles, they utilize the resource of protest much along the lines of Lipsky's model in the course of organizing, negotiations, and strike activities. During one set of negotiations with the Hartford Sheraton Hotel, union leaders sat in and were arrested at the main entrance to Aetna Insurance, which holds part interest in the hotel. The banks and insurance companies headquartered in Hartford seem especially averse to demonstrations taking place in front of their buildings, and the use of such a tactic by HERE does not go unnoticed by corporate officers who may be able to influence the process of contract negotiations at the hotel.

In addition to protest, the unions also engage in more routine political action to pursue objectives. In pursuit of union goals or in the course of solving union issues, 1199 regularly uses political channels, mobilizing members to contact and lobby public officials, and members turn out in en masse for hearings and other public meetings. HERE likewise mobilizes members to lobby, attend hearings, and other similar events. Both the UAW and 1199 have full-time lobbyists on their staffs, while HERE does not assign to any staff person that exclusive role.

Interunion and Intralabor Movement Relationships.   Interunion and internal labor movement relationships can either facilitate or impede goal attainment, through formal organizational structures and relationships, as well as through the norms articulated as labor movement values and serving as standards for behavior. Strike situations are useful illustrations.

Area unions who are conducting strikes often contact either the Greater Hartford Central Labor Council or the Connecticut State Labor Council—the federations of unions that are local and state arms of the AFL-CIO. Once a striking union contacts a local labor council, various activities may follow: monetary collections, mass picketing, rallies, contact with public officials, and other tactics. If the labor council participates in a community-labor alliance, that body may be approached, as previously described.

Unions expect such assistance because it is articulated as part of the raison d'être of local and state councils. Moreover, the norm of labor solidarity motivates participation, and such slogans as "An injury to one is an injury to all" are often seen on the placards or buttons of participants. Union members from other locals who attend or contribute to these efforts do so both to help fellow unionists and because they want to count on reciprocal assistance if they go on strike.

In addition to strike support, state and local labor councils may be called upon to provide assistance during organizing drives, and they may also engage in community service and political action programs. Political activities sometimes generate conflict when individual unions back different candidates vying for the same office. For example, in 1990, 1199 endorsed former Republican senator Lowell Weicker in his third-party bid for governor, despite the endorsement by the UAW and the rest of the LEAP forces of liberal former congressman Bruce Morrison. This action was greeted with great disappointment by other liberal left forces (Bass 1990).

Within this span of interunion contacts there are many points of contention, and sometimes the rivalries become quite intense. This is especially true of contested elections for AFL-CIO offices or floor fights at conventions on controversial resolutions. Additionally, the rift within the Democratic party between the more conservative faction and the progressive LEAP faction further divides the labor movement in its political activities.

One manifestation of these divisions surfaced over continued AFL-CIO support for the Colt strike for its four-year duration. Throughout the strike the UAW was not affiliated with the Connecticut State AFL-CIO, even though its international parent is affiliated nationally. When rallies were set or fund-raising appeals circulated, occasionally complaints would be heard at labor council meetings over giving continued assistance to a union that was not part of the AFL-CIO in Connecticut.

The internal labor movement divisions that are most significant for this analysis are those that revolve around the overall philosophy and vision of unions and the labor movement as a whole. The three unions in this study are among the activist unions that embrace both a larger, progressive social mission for the labor movement and an active, aggressive role for individual unions responding to the contemporary climate of industrial relations. This often brings them into conflict with the more conservative elements of the AFL-CIO.

Strike Strategies

There is probably nothing riskier in this era for unions than a strike, and a strike over economic issues alone is exceptionally difficult to win.

The Unfair Labor Practice Strategy.   Increasingly, unions are using the strategy of filing unfair labor practice charges with the NLRB against companies they strike. The intent is to transform economic strikes into unfair labor practices strikes in order to legally protect strikers' jobs from being filled by permanent replacements, assuming the charges are sustained through an NLRB trial. However, this strategy also involves risk: There is no guarantee that a union will win its case in the trial, and the time frame involved is usually quite lengthy. The NLRB trial in the Colt strike took over six months to conduct, and the decision was not rendered until more than one year later. During the agonizing wait for the verdict, strikers often expressed concern for the health and longevity of the judge.

The Lockout.   An auxiliary aspect of the unfair labor practices strike that sometimes allows strikers in Connecticut to receive unemployment benefits involves the strike's being designated as a lockout. Generally after some length of time on strike, the union makes an offer to return to work under the terms of the previous contract. If the company refuses, the union can then appeal to the Connecticut Labor Department to have the strike declared a lockout. In the case of a lockout, the workers who are prevented by the company from working may be eligible for unemployment compensation, and the amount of the unemployment benefit is generally greater than any union's strike benefit. Such a turn of events generally strengthens the case of the union with the NLRB since the union can claim that by not accepting the workers' offer, the company was not bargaining in good faith, an unfair labor practice. This strategy was pursued successfully during the Colt strike and in some of the 1199 strikes.

Dealing with Replacement Workers.   One of the most critical factors that makes strikes so difficult in recent years is the ease with which replacement workers have been hired. Winning a strike by setting up a picket line and expecting to halt production or service provision because no one will cross the line is now a virtual illusion for many segments of the labor movement, especially in situations where strikers are not engaged in highly skilled work.

Besides the capacity of firms in the manufacturing sector to move production activity to other sites, struck companies may take advantage of firms who recruit strikebreakers from other states, rendering the concept of community solidarity meaningless. Moreover, since the labor movement has undergone significant membership erosion in the past decade and unionized work sites have ceased operations in many cities, large segments of the work force—particularly younger workers—have no experience with unions and lack an understanding of the ethos of the labor movement around strikebreaking. Companies can readily exploit this situation.

Another example from the Colt strike demonstrates this phenomenon. Colt Firearms had approached the city of Hartford for Community Development Block Grant (CDBG) funds to assist in modernizing the Hartford plant before the onset of the strike. The company refused, however, to guarantee job slots for Hartford residents in exchange for the funding. The UAW supported the city's insistence on jobs for Hartford residents. However, once the strike began, Colt began recruiting replacement workers from among Hartford's unemployed and underemployed populations, particularly in the African American and Puerto Rican communities, the very residents the city wanted Colt to hire under the terms of the CDBG funding. The city decided to hold up any approval for

CDBG funds until the strike was settled. As detailed previously, the union and the Community-Labor Alliance were simultaneously approaching the neighborhood organizations and urging them to educate their constituencies about the issues of the strike. These constituencies included many individuals who had no experience with unions and simply saw an opportunity for employment.

The Corporate Campaign.   Since it is so difficult to win a strike on the picket line alone, in addition to the strategy of the unfair labor practices strike, unions are embracing what has become known as the corporate campaign. The term was first associated with the methodology of a particular individual, Ray Rogers, who worked with the J. P. Stevens boycott and Hormel strikers. It is now used more generically to refer to a strategy that attempts to discredit the struck company within the larger community and that also targets the company's financial base of support through such tactics as boycotts, attempting to halt third-party payments or government funding and contracts, pressuring the company's financiers, clients, or customers, and amassing political pressure on the company to settle, and other similar activities.

Many activities undertaken during the Colt strike, as previously discussed, conform to this corporate campaign strategy and will not be repeated here. However, both 1199 and HERE 217 have employed this type of strategy in the course of their strikes in recent years.

Buyouts and Employee Ownership Options.   The settlement of the Colt strike was fashioned around a unique set of circumstances which were never envisioned in the early years of the strike. As the strike wore on and the union's demands to halt Pentagon contracts until the strike was settled resulted in the Defense Department's awarding a contract for the M16 rifle to a competitor, it became clear that Colt was experiencing financial hardship. In April 1989, Colt Industries announced that it was putting the Firearms Division up for sale. The union first pursued a strategy of developing a proposal solely on its own for an employee ownership plan, but was later approached by an investor, Anthony Autorino. He asked them to consider a joint plan with other private investors and the state of Connecticut, which would be involved through the investment of pension funds. After months of extremely complicated negotiations, the deal was consummated in March 1990.

The new company that emerged, Colt Manufacturing Company, signed a collective-bargaining agreement with UAW Local 376, who also would have an 11 percent interest in the company. The settlement included raises and health benefits that would be fully paid by the company, two unsettled issues that had incited the strike in 1986. A $13 million settlement of back pay was agreed to by the union, with $10 million to be awarded immediately and $3 million in three years, assuming the new company was profitable. This back pay award is the largest in the history of the National Labor Relations Board.

The union takes immense pride in the settlement, something many even in the labor movement in Connecticut never expected to see. The model of part ownership by the union members, public pension fund involvement, and private investment will undoubtedly be studied and perhaps replicated elsewhere if appropriate factors converge. However, the entire venture is tremendously risky: First there is the problem of resecuring Defense Department contracts in an era of new spending patterns and reduced levels of defense funding. Next is the issue of the movement for greater gun control. At its opening, Colt Manufacturing was embroiled in a controversy over the sale of modified assault weapons to the public and had to attempt to maintain production of its Sporter rifle in the midst of the call for the banning of such weapons.

There is also the critical issue of former strikers' working with the former strikebreakers who were kept on the payroll of the new company. Shop floor interaction between these two groups during the first few months of operation of the new company was tense. Add to this the readjustment of workers who had been on a picket line, outside the regimentation and authority of factory operation for four years, as well as some dissension among different groups of former strikers, and the prospects for success of the new company become uncertain. Even though the strike was formally settled and the new company employs the former strikers, the impact of the strike will continue for a number of years as this new company cautiously carves out its existence.

The question of the company's financial viability became even more evident when in early 1992 it sought protection and reorganization under Chapter 11 bankruptcy proceedings. Several extensions were granted as the company has wound its way out of debt and into new production processes and product development.

Brinksmanship.   Often unions find themselves using brinksmanship strategies to attempt to achieve settlements. HERE in 1987 faced the possibility of strikes in three downtown Hartford hotels whose contracts had been negotiated purposely to expire at common deadlines so that the pressure from business clients of prospective strikes at major hotels would induce settlements. Last-minute settlements were obtained with two of the three hotels, and a four-month strike ensued at the Hartford Sheraton.

In recent years 1199 has used a brinksmanship approach in combination with pattern bargaining very publicly with both its nursing home division and its private sector/community-based mental health and retardation division. Its twenty-nine separate nursing home contracts have been negotiated to expire at roughly common deadlines, as have contracts for fourteen private sector mental health and retardation facilities and group homes. A key factor for both divisions is that the respective employers rely on reimbursements from various state agencies. As mentioned earlier, the union leadership relies on the state's being ill able to afford the chaos that strikes in a large number of nursing homes or group homes would bring, and the union therefore enjoys an advantage in such negotiations. In late 1989 with the nursing homes, and again in the summer of 1990 with the group homes, the union faced the prospect of strikes in over a dozen facilities at once. In both situations state funding was guaranteed and strikes were averted in all but one nursing home and in all of the private sector mental health and retardation facilities.

These negotiations were preceded by large spirited membership meetings where union members voiced overwhelming support for the strike option, if necessary. The group home workers meeting even included retarded clients, providing a poignant scene for the media of the relationship between the workers and their clients and the concern the workers experienced in feeling forced to consider striking. 1199 regularly attempts to highlight quality-of-care issues such as staffing patterns in its public relations efforts surrounding strikes or potential strikes, although the media does not always feature this aspect of the situation.

The gamble with this brinksmanship is that the tactic may force a union into an unwinnable strike and that eventually it may lose. In situations faced by HERE, where no state funds are involved, strikes may either eventually close down an establishment such as a restaurant or result in the end of the union shop at the site. 1199 has endured several strikes at nursing homes in which the facilities were ultimately closed because of problems with financing or because of a decision by the state. The unions feel that this may be an unfortunate but necessary consequence if they are ultimately to have the power to improve conditions for their members at other institutions.

Summary: Membership Mobilization

The work of any union centers on what is done to involve and serve its membership. The articulation of a union's mission and the philosophies and strategies that inform and guide its activities are critically important aspects of how workers experience union membership. Within the labor movement the distinction between those unions who envision their role as one of empowerment and those who define their role as providing a service to members is becoming a basis for deepening division. In varying degrees, I would assert that the three unions in this project fall on the empowerment side of the dichotomy; however, their risks and challenges are still formidable and they have suffered significant defeats nonetheless.

Empowerment in this instance may be interpreted in a number of ways: These unions all attempt to organize unorganized workers and are applying the new methodologies described in the first section of this chapter, forging models that other unions are also adopting. These unions also vigorously pursue raises in wages and improvements in working conditions during collective bargaining and will still go on strike as a last resort. They will employ protest when necessary, and also participate in electoral strategies that are not fail-safe. Perhaps most of all, they can be characterized as unions with leaders who are willing to take significant risks to advance their members' interests.

Many of labor's struggles can no longer be won on the basis of the union's own internal resources but require coordination with other unions and community forces, and the formulation of political strategies. These three unions are each attempting to fashion strategies to meet the difficulties of the contemporary labor relations environment through methods such as unfair labor practices strikes, corporate campaigns, the Colt buyout, new training activities for members in tackling shop floor issues, and the use of protest and political leverage in bold ways.

ORGANIZATIONAL STRUCTURE AND MAINTENANCE

Various aspects of the organization of a union may promote, hinder, or in some other way influence how the union accomplishes its goals. First, the organizational structures themselves may affect goal attainment. Moreover, as with corporations, unions are pursuing mergers and different forms of affiliations that influence effectiveness. Finally, organizational leadership is a key factor in success.

Organizational Structures

There are many common aspects of union structures: stewards, other officers and full-time functionaries, some type of work-site-based level of organization, and, except in the cases of local independent unions, some form of affiliation with a larger national or international structure. But there are also significant variations in structures that afford different models of accountability, different degrees of centralization or decentralization of authority and activity, and different degrees of membership participation in union affairs.

The UAW in Connecticut consists of approximately fifteen different union locals that are part of the regional apparatus of Region 9A. The constitution of the international union spells out various details of how union locals are to be organized: officer structures, certain financial and election procedures, and specially mandated committees. Within these constitutional provisions, however, each local has a great deal of autonomy in how it runs its affairs, and locals may adopt their own bylaws. Strike actions require the sanction of the international leadership in order for strikers to obtain strike benefits and other support.

The UAW's regional apparatus is an extension of the international organization headquartered in Detroit, as is the role of the regional director. The regional apparatus is not envisioned as another layer of organization to which locals affiliate and which in turn affiliates with the international; Rather, the regional apparatus *is* the international union, and therefore the regional director can be a pivotal actor in certain situations. In spite of the autonomy of UAW locals who at times remain aloof from the regional apparatus and carry on their affairs without much consultation, the regional director has important authority, especially in matters of strikes. The situation in Regional 9A at the beginning of the Colt strike vividly demonstrates this issue.

When UAW Local 376 struck Colt Industries in January 1986, the regional director of 9A at that time was E. T. "Ted" Barrett. The president of the local at the time was Phil Wheeler. Wheeler and Barrett had been rivals on internal union issues for a number of years. Although the strike at Colt received the sanction of the international union, Wheeler did not expect more than minimal assistance from Barrett in the impending difficult and lengthy strike. In order to have a better chance for success, the strike effort would need the full backing of the regional director to obtain the resources of the international, including support from the legal, research, and public relations divisions, as well as the capacity to make the strike a national priority of the union.

The constitutional convention of the UAW, at which regional directors are elected, was set for June of 1986. Early in the year, Region 9A CAP director John Flynn announced his candidacy for the position. Local 376 endorsed Flynn and participated in Flynn's successful campaign for the position, a campaign that emphasized the need to assist the Colt strike. Once elected, Flynn, who had less experience with negotiations and other shop issues than in the political action sphere, appointed Wheeler as assistant regional director. The assistant regional director position would assume greater prominence under Wheeler's tenure than was the case in previous administrations due to his experience with the more technical aspects of trade unionism, aspects that were often the basis of calls for assistance from union locals. Wheeler felt that from his new position he could provide greater assistance than as the local president to the strike effort by marshaling support within the region and at the international level.

In 1989, Flynn retired and Wheeler ran for regional director. After minimal initial opposition, Wheeler handily won unanimous election and several reelections. He has continued to carry out Flynn's political action agenda in the LEAP tradition and directed the process of union involvement in the buyout of Colt and the end of the strike. Had Flynn lost the 1986 bid, the entire course of events that culminated in the strike's conclusion might never have transpired, given the nature of the relationship of the local to the international union.

One other feature of UAW structure that exists in almost every other international union is that there are two types of union locals: locals that represent workers in only one shop or one employer with several sites, and amalgamated locals that represent workers with different employers, generally smaller work forces. This affords unions "economies of scale" in dealing with smaller workplaces or those where the work force is contracting. In situations where a work force has been reduced significantly, a local that was chartered for a single work site may merge into an amalgamated local to maximize union resources.

The structure of 1199 in New England resembles one large amalgamated local in that there are no separate union locals. Rather, each work site has a separate chapter but without the autonomy and constitutional or legal status of the locals of the UAW. The major unit of organization within 1199 has historically been the district level, and this is the only level below the national level set forth in the constitution of the National Union of Hospital and Health Care Employees, AFL-CIO which was in effect until the merger with Service Employees International Union (SEIU). There is a districtwide executive board made up of rank-and-file members who are elected by work sites.

This structure traces back to the time when 1199 was a local of the Retail, Wholesale and Department Store Union (RWDSU) and the membership was entirely within New York City. As the union grew outside the metropolitan New York area, the old Local 1199 subdivided, but into districts that were still technically divisions of the local. The merger with SEIU is requiring significant reorganization and will mean modification in this structure.

The district structure affords maximization of certain resources such as organizing and support staff, office and technical functions, educational programs, and other central functions. It also offers a more centralized authority structure, which can be important when dealing with employers. It would not make sense, for example, for each large state institution to have its own local and bargain separately for salaries and other matters when the personnel structure is one statewide system for all comparable state institutions. Likewise, the success in nursing home or private sector contract negotiations would be much more difficult with separate locals in each facility. Each chapter, however, does ratify the contract negotiated with its individual employer. One major benefit of the district structure, therefore, is the greater level of coordination.

Critics of such union structures maintain that large amalgamated organizations may be less democratic than smaller locals, that the leadership in these centralized structures possesses inordinate power, and that the large union organizations may become bureaucratic. 1199 in New England has grown dramatically in membership over the past fifteen years, especially after winning the right to represent state of Connecticut health care employees in 1978, and necessarily developed an organizational structure to accommodate this growth and the ensuing complexities of serving members in the state bureaucracy.

In 1975, the entire district staff of 1199 in New England could meet around a kitchen table, and organizers did all of the different tasks required by the union. Now the staff numbers close to forty people with distinct divisions of responsibilities. Union leaders maintain that the size and structure need not interfere with union democracy if the membership actively maintains involvement in union affairs and if the leadership stays in touch with the wishes of the members.

HERE's structure in the Hartford area combines elements of both the UAW and 1199. Local 217 is an amalgamated local with members in Hartford, New Haven, other Connecticut cities, Rhode Island, and parts of Massachusetts. When the Yale workers were organized, separate locals were chartered in order to effectively serve the concentration and specific needs of the membership at that institution. Local 217 has a staff of from five to eight people, assigned to work either on internal organizing in several different geographic areas or to new external organizing. External organizing is sometimes undertaken by a team of Local 217 and Local 34 organizers. As with 1199, each work site has its own union committee and "house" meetings of stewards are held monthly at the various work sites.

These varying structures afford different degrees of autonomy for the union organization at the work site level, which in and of itself is neither positive or negative. All three unions are tending toward larger units of organization. If there is any trade-off to be made, both union resource issues as well as the issue of strength in numbers tend to outweigh issues of autonomy. The tendency toward larger units of organization also manifests itself in the patterns of mergers and affiliations engaged in by these unions.

Mergers and Affiliations

The patterns of mergers and acquisitions in corporations have been the subject of much analysis and scrutiny in recent years. These activities often result in the concentration of capital and ever-increasing monopolization of the economy (Bluestone and Harrison 1982; and Harrison and Bluestone 1988). Among certain sectors of the labor movement, in order to increase their power and consolidate and maximize resources, a somewhat analogous process has begun. Although nowhere near as rapidly propelled as the activities of corporations, unions are deciding that there are major advantages to new combinations. Certain mergers and affiliations that were unimaginable within the labor movement as the Reagan era began are now either complete or under consideration: The Teamsters reaffiliated with the AFL-CIO, and the American Federation of Teachers and the National Education Association began cautiously discussing a possible future merger. The unions in Hartford are likewise involved in such developments.

Mergers. The National Union of Hospital and Health Care Employees, the parent union of 1199–New England, formally merged with Service Employees International Union (SEIU) in 1989. (To be more accurate, most of the National Union merged with SEIU.) This merger followed several years of dramatic dissension within the national union as the problem of finding a successor to the founding president of 1199, Leon Davis, unfolded with as many twists and turns as a television soap opera. In the end essentially three factions of 1199 existed: the New York membership—the union's original base that had grown to 70,000 members by the late 1980s—which remained affiliated for a time with RWDSU; the faction of the national union associated with Henry Nicholas, based mainly in his home district of Philadelphia and eastern Pennsylvania, which eventually merged with the American Federation of State, County and Municipal Employees (AFSCME); and the faction that took leadership from the New England district and its president, Jerome Brown, and former national executive vice-president Robert Muehlenkamp, roughly three-fourths of the National Union, which merged with SEIU.

It should be noted that earlier in the 1980s, a union with a heritage similar to 1199's, District 65 Wholesale and Warehouse Workers Union, also once a district of the RWDSU, affiliated with the UAW. The union then referred to itself as District 65 UAW. During Flynn's tenure as Region 9A director and continuing under Wheeler's, District 65 became fully integrated into the regional apparatus and finally disbanded as a separate entity. The other example of a merger within the UAW is that of IJAPA, discussed earlier.

Affiliations.   The UAW had not been affiliated with the AFL-CIO in Connecticut for several decades prior to 1990, though it was affiliated in other New England states. There was resistance in Connecticut among segments of UAW members, particularly those active in the CAP Council whose budget would be cut to pay affiliation fees to the state AFL-CIO and who would have to participate in the AFL-CIO Committee on Political Education (COPE), thereby losing the independence of the CAP. After several years of discussions and negotiations, and upon the completion of the Colt strike, the UAW did reaffiliate. It will be an important factor in statewide labor council elections and will have a substantial impact on the future direction of Connecticut's labor movement.

These examples of mergers and affiliations have arisen in response to the current economic climate and what is becoming more apparent in the larger labor movement, the need to consolidate and coordinate resources and activities. This pattern will merit close attention in the future to see what is successful in terms of accomplishing new goals and what merely creates larger but no more effective organizations. One factor that may be a useful indicator of the utility of such mergers is the amount of new organizing facilitated by the new arrangements: Will mergers indeed result in new resources sufficient to underwrite major organizing drives, or will the larger unions merely limp along and face continued membership erosion?

Leadership

While the constraints under which unions operate may flow from any combination of external problems, the subjective judgment of union leadership is also a critical variable in labor's response to its problems. The options and directions pursued by a union are very much products of the assessment of its leadership and the boldness with which the leaders answer demands.

Schwartz and Hoyman (1984) outline several challenges facing contemporary union leaders: representing members and relating to multiple constituencies such as other union leaders, union staff members, and political elites; technical competence in terms of legal pension, insurance, and other issues; and management of union bureaucracies. Union presidents are often considered the "chief bargainer" for their unions in key sets of negotiations and may be significant actors in national and regional political scenes. The job of a contemporary union leader is immensely complex, vastly underrecognized and hardly ever rewarded with public acclaim.

One feature—extremely unquantifiable—in terms of individual leadership qualities is the phenomenon of leadership charisma. Charisma in this instance includes the knowledge, judgment, honesty, dauntlessness, and commitment that foster membership confidence and trust. In all three organizations, certain unique qualities of one or more leaders have immense impact on the ability of the union to wage and win struggles.

Certainly within the UAW, Phil Wheeler's leadership is recognized in this light. The tenacity of the Colt strikers was in part attributable to their willingness to follow his direction and their faith that ultimately he would fashion a way out of their dilemma. By some estimations the strikers came to rely too heavily on him, expecting miracles.

Wheeler is a self-taught union leader who worked at Colt and spent eighteen years as president of Local 376. Union staff members relish telling stories of how he knows labor law so well that he directs the union lawyers to pursue strategies the lawyers themselves are unable to conceive. However, Wheeler is also extremely amenable to suggestions from forces outside the UAW, as was the case in the Colt strike. Wheeler is relentless in pursuit of the goals he defines for the union, and there is also a very pragmatic aspect of his leadership that can engage in the minute technical details of very specific plans. Though not formally schooled in radical political-economy, in many ways he conforms to Antonio Gramsci's notion of the organic intellectual, an individual who rises to leadership from the ranks of the working class.

The leaderships of 1199 and HERE Local 217 come from different backgrounds and origins, as activists who entered the labor movement from a political commitment to social change. The generation of leadership in both of these unions today traces back to the social activism of the 1960s combined with concrete experiences under the tutelage of many older activists who helped to build their respective unions. 1199–New England president Jerome Brown "apprenticed" with the late 1199 president and founder Leon Davis; former HERE 217 secretary-treasurer Henry Tamerin and other 217 staff with the late Vincent Sirabella, who became the organizing director of HERE's International. Other leaders in both unions come not only from rank-and-file activists, but also largely from the ranks of former student, community, civil rights, and women's movement activists from the movements of the 1960s and 1970s. What distinguishes many of these individuals from their more conservative contemporaries in other unions are both their more radical ideologies and sense of purpose for the labor movement, and their personal commitment and efforts as they work long hours for relatively modest salaries.

The collective talent of 1199's staff is impressive and has fanned out into other areas: Its former secretary-treasurer served as a deputy labor commissioner in Connecticut; a former vice-president is currently a state representative; a current vice-president is secretary-treasurer of LEAP. Moreover, in the midst of the dearth of new organizing of the 1980s, 1199–New England maintained its commitment to organizing the unorganized and achieved greater success in their organizing endeavors than most other unions. And despite some crushing defeats, 1199 has been known as a union that will

"fight the good fight." The 1990 Weicker endorsement may ultimately somewhat tarnish the union's image, however, in light of the
rocky first term of the Weicker administration in handling Connecticut's fiscal crisis.

These unique sets of leaders influence their respective unions
quite distinctively: From Phil Wheeler has come the carefully crafted
unfair labor practices strike strategy and the Colt buyout; from
Jerry Brown and his colleagues have come bold, militant actions
both in strikes and contract negotiations, and new standards of
public employee unionism; from Local 217 has come militancy and
determination to take on some of the most powerful downtown
corporate interests in Hartford and organize extremely difficult and
transient work sites. The presence of these various actors has an
almost serendipitous quality: It is difficult to imagine the various
successes of these unions without these specific leaders in their
specific roles. In this sense the unique or charismatic leader is an
important factor in understanding how these labor unions fashion
strategies in the current economic climate.

CONCLUSIONS

In many ways the challenges these unions face in the contemporary labor relations climate feel to their leaderships like changes in
the levels of difficulty they have always encountered. Employers
may have become more brazen in their tactics to curb unions'
power, but they have always resisted unionization. The unions
therefore have had to become more steeled in their own determination. Some of their tactics are more of a "last resort" type—using
the NLRB to win strikes, participating in a company buyout—
strategies they would not have pursued if winning a strike on a
picket line alone was still in any way a possibility. Other tactics
involve more sophisticated uses of activities they have historically
involved themselves in, but which today are more strategically
important in their work. An important example is their willingness
to involve themselves more deeply in the political process by
participating in organizations such as LEAP or People for Change,

as well as enhancing their own internal mechanisms for political action.

One of the most difficult areas for the unions today is organizing. In the contemporary climate, organizing the unorganized requires more careful selection of work sites, refinement of targeting and identifying work site leadership and more intense preparation with the organizing committee. Besides developing the appropriate models or techniques such as 1199's Blitz or HERE's 1-2-3, the unions are also challenged to devote sufficient resources and structure their organizations in such a way as to facilitate organizing. All have assigned specific personnel to this function or reorganized their staffing patterns to accommodate new organizing.

The major problem that the unions face is what we identified earlier: The system of labor law in the United States no longer facilitates worker organization. The NLRB has ceased to be a vehicle to ensure workers' rights, but instead is itself a battleground. Its processes are lengthy and cumbersome, a factor that alone can dampen organizing potential and that is exploited by employers as they attempt to stall organizing drives. NLRB processes also tend to prolong any strikes that are being adjudicated through NLRB trials, and especially if companies are operating with replacement workers, the union strikers are placed at a distinct disadvantage. Employers flagrantly violate labor law with a type of impunity that the lengthy processes of adjudication allow.

As labor's power has eroded at the labor board, so has its power with employers and its respect in the community. Accordingly, what has functioned in the past as a community solidarity ethos that militates against strikebreaking has also seriously eroded. Unions are trying to recapture community support by developing corporate campaigns and attempting to place their particular struggles with employers into larger community contexts through such vehicles as community-labor alliances.

Responding to these developments requires membership involvement and cultivation. These unions engage their shop floor and work site leaders in training exercises to prepare them for shop floor issues. The memberships hear organizational points of view that are critical of corporate power, but the range of ideologies varies among the three from the UAW's more social democratic themes to HERE 217's and 1199's more radical articulation of class relationships. Beyond the themes stressed in organizational activities and publications, opportunities for involvement are afforded in public events such as rallies, hearings, and political action, and sometimes disruptive tactics are employed.

Leadership and structure are important ingredients in the effectiveness of modern unionism and vary among the three unions of this study. 1199's centralized structure and HERE 217's amalgamated structure afford coordination but vest a great deal of power in district leadership. The autonomy of the UAW's locals offers opportunities for different patterns of interplay between "layers" of the union, and the regional director, similar to 1199–New England's president or HERE 217's secretary-treasurer, has great influence over the course of union issues.

Finally, the individual qualities of the leaders themselves significantly shape the directions of the unions. Based on the different experiences and standards of judgment used by their respective leaders, these three unions vary in the paths they take toward their goals of membership empowerment. Each provides innovative examples of contemporary unionism, and each is being observed with great interest in Connecticut's labor movement as well as the larger movement for social change.

Some of the adjustments these unions are making to accommodate the present labor relations climate provide new models of membership empowerment but others seem like attempts simply to hold on by whatever means are available. Yet, some of their struggles are logged in the "loss" column.

At a time when the system of labor law seems to be failing unions quite miserably, use of these laws appears to be one of the few major avenues that remains available to unions in such efforts as difficult strikes. Another important avenue is to recreate a public opinion climate that is more supportive of unions, leading ultimately to legislation that is more supportive of unionization. Toward this end the community-labor alliances, political action, and other extraorganizational activities, along with an activated, involved, and adroit membership, are important tools and strategies for union survival and growth.

Neighborhood Organizing

Neighborhood organizers in Hartford take great pride in the degree of community organization in the city. In many cities, there are a few neighborhoods with some type of community or neighborhood organization, but most of the city remains unorganized. In Hartford, the opposite is true: Most areas are within the "turf" of one of the neighborhood organizations, residents can call upon the organization, and this arrangement encourages more organization. Not all of the various groups or associations follow in the Alinsky or neo-Alinsky tradition, but the three largest, Asylum Hill Organizing Project (AHOP), Organized North Easterners–Clay Hill and North End (ONE-CHANE), and Hartford Areas Rally Together (HART), in some measure each trace their methodologies and philosophies back to the Alinsky legacy of block-level organizing, bold confrontational tactics with public and corporate officials, and the garnering of tangible, specific victories.

The three Hartford-based organizations have existed long enough to evolve along distinct paths, according to the needs of the different neighborhoods in which they function and the orientations of their respective staffs and local neighborhood leaders. These differences have influenced their respective responses to economic restructuring.

As profiled earlier, the logic of neighborhood organizing as it exists in most locations, and particularly in Hartford, is quite different from the logic of labor organizing. No ready separation exists between organizing new members and working with existing membership for the neighborhood organizations. There is no formal membership status based on legally defined procedures such as elections, no payment of dues as a condition of membership, and virtually no way to distinguish members from nonmembers. Essentially, there are only active participants in issues and campaigns undertaken by the organization. Therefore, recruiting new participants and maintaining the interest of the old participants is in reality one activity, with leadership development receiving a great deal of emphasis. Moreover, because the work with participants involves a process of continually organizing, the issues of organizational structure and maintenance are critical to the life of the organizations.

ORGANIZING AND MOBILIZING

Neighborhood organizing in Hartford has resulted in many achievements, and this success has led to the near institutionalization of the entire process. Who participates, the issues focused on, how the organizing is effected, the organizational points of view and philosophies, and the manner in which the issues addressed by the groups embody responses to restructuring all set the tone for local neighborhood organizing.

Participants and Issues

When one thinks of community activism, there is often a mental picture of the militant young people of the 1960s demanding a share of resources and inclusion in public decision making. But the activists of Hartford's neighborhood organizations are a very different set of actors from those in the picture during the 1960s. Issues like crime and health care attract property owners, small-business owners, and senior citizens, and the issue of education draws parents, many of whom are young single mothers. Tenant rights and housing issues bring a broad range of individuals to the groups. Participants may be motivated as much by fear as by the desire to upgrade their standard of living.

While widespread poverty exists in Hartford, there is variation among the neighborhoods in terms of the degree of poverty, and these variations sometimes manifest themselves in the work of the neighborhood organizations both in relation to who participates and the nature of the issues addressed. For example, ONE-CHANE operates in the northern part of the city, an area with large concentrations of public housing (although ONE-CHANE refrains from organizing in public housing where active tenants organizations in exist), and whose population is almost exclusively African American and Puerto Rican, many of whom are very poor. HART operates in the southern part of the city, which contains the remaining enclaves of white ethnic groups, a surging Puerto Rican and Latino population, and increasing numbers of African Americans and Asians. Although poverty exists in HART's turf, many of its neighborhoods are relatively better off than those of the other two organizations. So while HART activists attempted to stop the establishment of a "Chucky Chicken" fast-food/convenience store in order to preserve the character of a neighborhood during 1989, several years earlier ONE-CHANE activists attempted to extract commitments for jobs for area residents from the developer of a Burger King franchise who opened a restaurant in their neighborhood.

In the early years of the respective organizations, a great deal of effort went into establishing block club levels of organization. Organizers spent much of their time going door to door, talking to residents, trying to ascertain which issues were important to these residents. Efforts were then made to bring residents together to discuss problems and define courses of action. This was and remains a slow, painstaking process. And although it is still employed by the organizations in some situations, they now have sufficient histories and track records to vary their methods. Accordingly, HART now works more directly with the churches in its neighborhoods, establishing contact with their clergy and, through these clergy, the parishioners. The organizations also make extensive use of the large mailing lists they have amassed over the years, augmented by telephone contact, as a method of organizing. Furthermore, now many community residents approach the organizations with their concerns rather than waiting for an organizer to come to their neighborhood.

Within the organizations are different task forces and committees that focus on specific issues. The individual activists may change over time, and various dimensions of the issues may evolve so that the committees themselves look quite different from year to year. As an illustration, AHOP has dealt with the issue of crime essentially since its inception. In 1987 and 1988, AHOP activists from the group's anticrime committee defined the issue in terms of demands for more police officers in the neighborhood, redeployment of police from the Colt picket line to the neighborhoods, and the deployment and full staffing of police foot patrols. By 1990, with the crime-drug nexus producing an escalating public safety crisis, the crime issue took the form of debate over whether to call the Guardian Angels into the neighborhood, and a different group of individuals were involved from those of two to three years earlier.

One of the primary methodological approaches of these organizations is the articulation of issues as specific and tangible demands that can be fought for and won. Organizers characterize this as turning a problem into an issue: A problem may be something extremely general or global, but an issue is something specific around which a group can mobilize. One of the roles of the organizer is to help a group delineate an issue or set of issues from a larger problem. These issues must be amenable to actions in which the organization articulates one or more demands. Hence the crime issue became defined in terms of a demand for foot patrols.

A secondary objective of this methodology is that in time the neighborhood activists will develop more sophisticated analyses and be able to tackle more complex issues. This type of growth occurred within HART's anticrime committee. When it became apparent that foot patrols alone would not provide an ultimate solution to crime, participants in the anticrime committee began to consider the issue from a more systemic perspective and developed a comprehensive anticrime proposal that combined drug education and treatment options with youth recreation programming, community policing, and other crime control measures. In working on this issue with such specific demands, the participants recognized the need for this broader perspective and recognized the effectiveness of comprehensive measures to address crime.

Most issues remain at a more simplified level of analysis, however. Unless participants work with issues over an extended period—several years, as illustrated in the crime issue example—there is a need on the part of the organizations to distill issues into "winnable" items. Moreover, when neighborhood residents are approached by or call upon organizers, often their concerns are about very local matters: the street light that is not working, the potholes in the road, the lack of traffic control signs, the overflowing dumpster down the street, and so on. Developing the capacity of neighborhood residents to move beyond the "street-light and pothole stage" requires a great deal of effort by organizers and considerable amounts of time. And, if this development is achieved with one group of activists, still newer participants are being recruited into other organizational endeavors so that simplified issues must always be a part of the organizations' agenda.

These organizations tend to focus on issues of social consumption, often expressed as conflict relating to the service delivery system of the local government. In many instances organizational activity revolves around local public bureaucracy: pressuring the city government to take action against owners of abandoned buildings or to enforce building codes; pressuring the school board to allocate more supplies to schools; lobbying the city council to maintain services involving items such as garbage collection from small businesses or to adopt particular forms of property tax relief; and, of course, pressuring the police department to deal more effectively with crime control.

At other times specific individuals in the private sector become targets: slumlords, bank officials, or a hospital's community relations representative. However, even though the targets may operate within the private sector, pressures brought to bear on them may often be orchestrated through municipal agencies: If the slumlord will not accede to the demands of the tenants who are organized by one of the neighborhood organizations, the tenants will then approach various municipal agencies to take action in the situation or eventually take the issue into the judicial system, although, as detailed in the chapter on coalitions, the neighborhood organizations try to avoid reliance on the legal system or attorneys if at all possible.

As mentioned earlier, the participants vary with the issues. Organizers characterize self-interest as the key motivation for participation and view their job as tapping that self-interest. Many older homeowners, on fixed incomes, both African American and white, participate in order to preserve a standard of living that they perceive as rapidly slipping from their grasp. Younger participants who are effectively the indigenous leaders in their neighborhoods are also involved in the activities. Sometimes very specific issues generate participation: tenants who have nowhere else to turn in dealing with problem landlords or small-business people who are drawn to the organizations because of the crime issue. There are also individuals who contact an organization with a specific request for information and become drawn into the group's work. This was how one former president of AHOP was introduced to the group, by inquiring about summer youth employment options for her children. Certain services provided by the organizations function as incentives to bring people into the groups, and these will be described later. Participation in the organizations promotes the growth of "other-centered" behavior, and initial self-interest may be transformed into broader concern and involvement in the larger community.

Process of Neighborhood Organizing

A process of leadership development and consensus formation through group decision making generally precedes any appearance by neighborhood activists at public meetings. The elements of the process include the leaders, the organizer, the planning activities, and the chosen strategy and tactics.

Leaders. Neighborhood residents or other participants in the organizations who develop into leaders are critical to the success of any group effort. Similar to the way in which union organizers define what constitutes a leader, neighborhood organizers define leaders as people with constituencies and, very critically, credibility with their constituencies. Leaders need not be the loudest, most articulate, or best-liked person in a group, but it is important that leaders motivate others to participate and that they themselves take on tasks and responsibilities, including the mundane work the organization must engage in: preparing the leaflets, calling other participants, setting up meetings, and other similar activities. In many situations it is important for leadership to be collective in nature, especially among low-income constituencies where problems of survival and everyday living may become major impediments to participation.

Organizers describe a type of screening process for emerging leaders in which, after having developed and maintained followings, they assume responsibilities that demonstrate their reliability and stamina. However, there is also extensive leadership training by the organization, some of it in actual workshop sessions and some on a one-to-one basis between organizers and leaders.

Leadership training focuses on organizational needs such as the ability to approach neighborhood residents to discuss issues, as well as the ability to mobilize people, to run meetings, and to make issues appealing to the organization's constituencies. Training also involves analytical tasks such as strategy development, analysis of power relationships in order to determine targets' pressure points, and ways of presenting issues to the media and the general public. An extremely important element in the entire range of training activities is the development of personal confidence on the part of the potential leaders. The issue of how participating in the organizations facilitates personal empowerment of women and people of color, in particular, arises in any discussion of neighborhood organizing with organizers or leaders.

The one-on-one work with organizers is often the most intensive type of leadership training. Organizers describe a process in which they may eventually develop a very collegial relationship with the neighborhood leaders, engaging in mutual give and take in deciding upon strategy and tactics. The organizer's role, therefore, is also extremely critical to the success of the organizations.

Organizers.   The role of the organizer in neighborhood organizing is multidimensional. Veteran Hartford neighborhood leader and now organizing consultant Alta Lash of United Connecticut Action for Neighborhoods, Inc. (UCAN), characterizes the role as being both a catalyst and a manager of action. Organizers must have many of the same qualities as leaders—credibility, integrity, and an ability to inspire confidence and action—but they must also know how to step back and allow the leaders to lead. There can be a thin line between prodding or challenging a leader and directing the leader or the rest of the group, something an organizer is essentially prohibited from doing either formally by the organizations or implicitly in the ethos and models that inform the groups' practice.

The power of neighborhood organizers to manipulate situations or individuals is sometimes voiced as a methodological criticism of Alinsky-style neighborhood organizing. The criticism is based on the fact that neighborhood organizations claim to be democratically controlled by neighborhood residents and other participants who are supposed to set direction, rather than the organizers. Yet often just at a moment when a meeting may be turning in one direction, an organizer can inject a comment or suggestion that can turn the meeting in an entirely different direction. The suggestion may be quite subtle, but it still can change the discussion substantially.

Organizers counter this criticism by maintaining that neighborhood people cannot be persuaded to take actions for which they are unprepared, and they will not remain involved with the organizations if they feel they have no control over organizational direction.

Organizers assert that it is their job to provide suggestions and stimulate discussion of different options, that it is their role to provide a menu of options in a given situation and assist neighborhood residents in working through these choices. They are also the people who must come up with new strategies when setbacks or defeats occur.

The development of individuals into competent organizers may take several years and is a process built upon the trials and errors of on-the-job training. A great deal of subjective assessment is required in situations where there is not necessarily a right or wrong way to proceed, but rather a more or less effective way that may not be known in advance. There are formal workshops or training sessions for organizers, but much of their development comes through supervision and consultation with their directors or consultants such as the UCAN staff. Moreover, capitalizing on individual strengths and learning to feel comfortable in the role of organizer are also important.

Planning and Orchestrating Issues.   The orchestration of an issue campaign involves several stages of planning by organizers and leaders, at each stage broadening the level of participation by interested neighborhood residents. A typical scenario is illustrated by the AHOP senior group as they took up the issue of crime in the summer of 1987. In this situation, initial discussions take place between an organizer and one or two leaders to chart a preliminary course of action. A planning committee is then assembled, ranging in size from six to ten people to affirm the direction and take responsibility for specific tasks. The individuals who chair the planning meetings spend a great deal of time with organizers in constructing the agenda. Little is left to chance, and these meetings have a fairly fixed format with detailed lists of what must be done.

If after routine contact is made with local officials by the neighborhood group committee through telephone conversations or in person, and requests are met with inaction, one likely strategy is to organize a community meeting in which someone with authority in the issue (such as a city official) is invited to answer questions or respond to demands. There is a standardized agenda used in most of the community meetings—accountability sessions, as they are often called—which is both straightforward and very helpful in keeping the meeting focused on the intended objectives. There is great potential for these meetings to get sidetracked on tangential issues, and the leader must have a specific agenda to keep the larger group on track. The agenda outline may be as follows:

Introduction

Statement of the issues: background and facts

Presentation of demands

Response from guest(s) (the guest may then be asked to leave)

Discussion of next steps

This agenda format is used by leaders and groups who are experienced, unified on an issue, and adept at asserting demands, as well as by leaders and groups who are not particularly well organized or articulate. With the more experienced groups, the organizers play a minimal role and stay more in the background. With the less experienced leaders and groups, the organizers tend to assert themselves at key points to keep the group focused and help move the meeting along.

Despite all of the careful planning, sometimes spontaneity reigns and totally unanticipated actions take place at meetings. One such event transpired on August 6, 1987, when AHOP's Housing Coalition met to discuss the next steps in dealing with a recalcitrant landlord who refused to properly maintain or take action to stem drug dealing in his buildings. As tenants related horrifying stories of fires in the buildings, intimidation by drug dealers, and absolute refusal on the part of the landlord to make repairs, anger and outrage among the rest of the meeting participants grew. The plans to take the landlord to court or attempts to find buyers for the buildings seemed too remote—the group felt the need to do something at that moment.

On the agenda were items that suggested having local police and state housing and banking officials tour the buildings and see firsthand the disgusting conditions that the tenants were enduring. The group decided that rather than wait until the future for such a building tour, they would go to the police station that night and demand that the police take action on the drug dealing. They called a local television station to obtain media coverage of the action and particularly to have a public record of the police department's response. The group, which included several small children, piled into AHOP's vans and several individuals' cars, drove to the police station, met with the night sergeant, and voiced their complaints.

The sergeant attempted to placate the group by stating that he would have officers look into the problems, but he also presented various reasons why little had been, or could be, done. This further angered the group, and even the otherwise low-profile organizers entered into the heated discussion. A television news crew arrived and filmed some of the interchange, which appeared on the 11 P.M. news.

In this instance, there were no immediate effects as a result of the spontaneous action, but there was a sense of emotional release for the group and the tenants could at least feel that they had supporters and had in some measure asserted themselves. Moreover, the media coverage helped in the continuing orchestration of the issue. Eventually—much later—the landlord sold the buildings.

Spontaneity may also lead to situations where events get out of control for the organization. On August 1, 1990, HART's tax committee called a meeting in a South End church to discuss the property tax revaluations that had taken place over the previous year. Homeowners were in the process of paying new, substantially larger tax bills, and complaints were being heard all over the city. At the HART meeting one of the city's tax officials was present to answer questions and discuss the various options for tax relief that were available to residential property owners. Several residents whose English-speaking abilities were limited started screaming at the official and grew so impatient that they rushed the podium and attempted to wrestle the microphone from the HART president, who was chairing the meeting. Although the president kept physical control of the microphone, the decorum of the meeting was never fully restored.

Most of the meetings held by these organizations proceed as originally intended, more often characterized by solid planning and sometimes a tenor that seems almost rehearsed. A frequently employed tactic involves some type of guerilla theater skit or a satirical presentation to a public official of items symbolic of the issue at hand. The opening pages of this book recount AHOP's delivering uncollected garbage from a slumlord's building to the Hartford city manager's office (the same slumlord was the focus of the sortie to the police department described above). During the linkage struggle in 1986, the organizations presented the city council with a skeleton that was missing its spine—an attempt to dramatize what they characterized as the spinelessness of the council in acceding to the corporate community by voting down the linkage proposals.

Satire and comedy can be used effectively by the groups to make various points to the public, but also to reduce fears on the part of neighborhood residents. Organizers maintain that if residents can feel a degree of humor and lightheartedness in some of the events in which they participate, the fear of participating and speaking out may diminish in the lighter atmosphere. In Hartford, the effective use of humor has evolved over the history of the three organizations, fueled by the skills and wit of various organizers. This tactic is advocated in many national training workshops and in manuals and books on neighborhood organizing (see Kahn 1982, 196).

One of the most formidable challenges in an issue campaign for the neighborhood organizations is deciding on new tactics or next steps in difficult struggles. Winning is very important, not merely in and of itself, but also in maintaining the interest and involvement of neighborhood residents. Therefore, choosing strategies and tactics is critical not only to organizational effectiveness but also to continued participation.

Strategies and Tactics. Decisions on strategies and tactics take into account: the issue of unpredictability, the use of media coverage, the personalization of organizing targets, the use of confrontation and anger, and the interplay of the groups' campaigns with politics.

One rule of thumb of neighborhood organizers is to maintain unpredictability. The object is to keep organizing targets off balance and unable to plan their responses to the actions of the groups. One of the major advantages of this tactic is greater control of media coverage through the element of surprise. Neighborhood groups want to set the tone and not allow the target an opportunity for advance preparation, but rather place him or her in the position of scurrying to fashion a response to unexpected developments. This relates to another key ingredient in the organizations' issue campaigns, media coverage.

Media coverage, coupled with the element of surprise, supports Lipsky's (1970) model of protest as an apt analysis of how the neighborhood organizations fashion strategies. If one accepts staged actions such as the guerilla theater skits mentioned previously as protest, as well as protest with a genuinely angry flavor, then it is possible to view a large portion of the public actions of the neighborhood groups as attempts to activate what Lipsky refers to as the targets' "reference publics" (the larger audience to whom the target feels accountable or who can bring pressure on the target). Media coverage is a critical component of such a strategy. In Hartford, the neighborhood organizations receive a great deal of media coverage of their public activities.

In as many instances as possible neighborhood organizers prefer to personalize a campaign and single out one individual as a target. Rather than deal with an entire corporation such as a bank, a particular bank officer or representative is held accountable. The same strategy is applied to city bureaucrats or elected officials:

Individuals who have the power to make decisions or take actions are made the specific targets. On the one hand this helps concretize the problem for neighborhood residents—anger can be directed to a real human being. On the other hand, even if the targeted person resists initially, he or she may eventually tire of the attention and give in to the group's demands. During the Colt strike it was a neighborhood organizer in the Community-Labor Alliance who suggested using the president of Colt Firearms as the target of a protest campaign.

It may appear that organizations in the Alinsky mold often rush to confrontational tactics, that there is a penchant for confrontation on the part of these groups. Indeed, to this author, one of the most striking aspects of their work, which helped inspire this project, is the way in which through participation in these organizations, neighborhood people without a great deal of experience in public affairs come to the point where they will boldly confront a corporate or public official. Yet, in reality, confrontational situations are not as routine for these organizations as one might expect, despite the groups' reputations and the ever-present threat felt by local policymakers that such tactics could be used.

Before any of the neighborhood organizations' committees or other formations arrive at a point where they undertake a confrontation, they generally attempt more routine methods of alleviating their problems. They will patiently call a city official and set up a group meeting, which may be conducted quite civilly. If they achieve the desired end, then the organization claims a victory and the group can move on to other issues. However, the kind of stalling tactics that may be employed by bureaucrats or the indifference that a group may encounter even from elected officials can be used by organizers to kindle anger. Without the support of a neighborhood organization, anger might never be cultivated and put to any strategic use, and individuals would merely become cynical about the possibility for change. But these organizations use anger as a motivational force in their campaigns and educate leaders in the use of anger as part of issue orchestration.

Organizers assert that it takes an incredible amount of disregard and neglect to get ordinary people angry enough to engage in confrontation with public officials, that such behavior is not generally within their experience. So, at key points in campaigns, when organizers sense that the residents are "ready"—sufficiently fed up—they begin to channel the anger to generate confrontation. Recognizing when this point has been reached is something organizers learn through experience; it involves a very subjective assessment on the organizer's part.

Even though these neighborhood organizations do not engage in partisan politics through such vehicles as political action committees, they regularly make demands on elected officials and, therefore, command a distinct presence in local politics. Sometimes they attempt to put a politician on the spot and extract a commitment in a public forum to a specific position or a particular vote. At other times they meet with officials in more private settings to discuss issues or jointly develop strategies in a more cooperative atmosphere.

Organizational Messages and Media

The leadership of the neighborhood organizations articulate their ideologies in vague or amorphous terms. They are highly pragmatic in pursuing goals: They explicitly espouse general concepts such as empowerment and participatory democracy while they implicitly embrace a principle of localism. Organizers refrain from stating their own views in ideological terms, especially any that reflect a leftist perspective, in part to avoid alienating contributors and in part because the written materials produced by the groups tend to focus on specific issues without a philosophical or ideological analysis.

Empowerment and Participatory Democracy.   While an argument can be made that the existence of the neighborhood groups channels discontent into manageable patterns (analogous to characterizations of modern unionism as disciplining labor), the individuals who establish, staff, and assume leadership in the organizations do so with sincere intentions to effect change and redefine power relationships in local communities, with great personal effort and sacrifice. The rewards for participation are seldom of a monetary nature, except perhaps when an issue involves taxation and participants expect to save money on tax bills, or when pressure is exerted on a bank to provide low-interest loans. The staffs of the organizations earn very modest salaries, and the neighborhood people who participate are all volunteers.

The theme of community empowerment therefore appears to have resonance and motivate participation, especially when it builds upon and combines with the different types of self-interest that exist in the neighborhoods. Certainly the continuing existence of HART since 1975 is one indication of both the appeal of neighborhood organizing in the community and the tenacity of the organizers and neighborhood leadership.

Article III in AHOP's bylaws, which defines the purpose of the organization, helps illustrate how the mission of community empowerment is conceived:

ARTICLE III   *Purpose*
SECTION 1
The purpose of AHOP, as a non-profit community organization, shall be to establish an organization whereby the various age, ethnic, racial, and economic groups within the neighborhood can come together and address their concerns through a democratic process.
SECTION 2
AHOP shall be the uniting vehicle whereby the community, as a whole, can work together to improve the quality of life in the neighborhood.
AHOP shall, through its member groups and the Board, organize and mobilize residents in the neighborhood, empowering them through a process of democratic decision-making

and direct action to address particular issues affecting the
quality of life in the neighborhood. AHOP shall, through its
member groups and the Board, develop and implement service
delivery programs that strive to strengthen the bonds of
community and create a healthy functioning neighborhood.
(By-Laws, May 1987)

How this is interpreted and what is meant by empowerment
takes many forms. On one level, the simple act of participating in a
neighborhood issue by attending a meeting can be conceived as
empowerment in that by their attendance, residents are taking an
interest and a role, however minimal, in community affairs. That
the organizations hold meetings on community issues means that
local government or private interests often have to factor the
responses of the neighborhood groups into their plans for the
respective neighborhoods. Achieving such a result is considered by
the organizations as an indication of success and a measure of
empowerment.

Besides this "watchdog" effect, empowerment encompasses both
tangible improvements in the community, as well as avenues for the
less tangible benefits of personal growth and development. In
relation to actual physical development, all three neighborhood
organizations have been involved in the housing arena: AHOP
established Hill Housing, Inc., in the late 1980s; HART, along with
several other organizations, helped to establish the Broad-Park
Development Corporation in the early 1980s (although it has at
times experienced differences with the corporation over its direction
and priorities); and ONE-CHANE's staff functions include housing
development. All three hold periodic housing fairs to disseminate
information on home ownership opportunities. Any new housing
that is developed through their efforts fills a very dire need in and of
itself, and also tangibly demonstrates the value of the organizations
for the neighborhoods' improvement.

The avenues for personal development have been mentioned in
the earlier discussion of leadership, but here it can be emphasized

that growth on a personal level by individual participants simultaneously builds new local leadership, cultivates organizational loyalty, and contributes to greater overall organizational effectiveness. Moreover, as other community residents watch their neighbors undergo this personal empowerment, and as new role models emerge in the neighborhoods, the organizations' stature is often enhanced in the process. Organizers point to the development of local leadership as an important component of community empowerment.

Notwithstanding criticisms of the neighborhood organizations in which they are characterized as being led, and worse, manipulated, by staff, it can still be argued that they do provide people at the grassroots level opportunities for participation in political and economic developments. The claims that they build structures for participatory democracy can be examined both in terms of internal processes and external effects.

Internally, formal control is exerted by neighborhood residents through the annual election of the organizations' boards of directors and the process of selecting organizational priorities at annual congresses. Theoretically, priorities are set at these congresses when participants are asked to vote for the issues they feel are most important for organizational attention from a list of potential issues. The items with the highest number of votes are then taken up by the board of directors and the various committees for development of plans and campaigns.

Many other issues arise during any given year, but the priority list is used as an indication of what is most important to area residents. However, neighborhood residents also exercise control over the organizations' respective agendas simply by demonstrating interest or disinterest in particular issues through indicators such as meeting attendance and follow-through on group decisions. If there is a lack of interest, the organizations will not expend resources to pursue an issue.

The creation of avenues for greater citizen participation in community decisions is another effect of the organizations' existence. Separate from any question of internal organizational democracy, building these avenues is perhaps the more compelling motivation for organizers. It is what organizers envision in their conceptualization of democratic participation in decision making: community input into those decisions that affect community life. In terms of external effects, the organizations attempt to counter government insensitivity or incompetence and sometimes the power of private corporate interests in the community. This function is not necessarily articulated by organizers in strong ideological or conceptual terms, but more in terms of the groups' day-to-day activities and the tenor of the issue campaigns that they organize.

In talking to organizers and executive directors of the organizations, it is often difficult to elicit an articulation of the mission or function of their groups in greater detail than a very general notion of empowerment or participatory democracy. Because of the myriad demands on them, they necessarily function very pragmatically and are preoccupied with day-to-day operations and the need to build the capabilities of the organizations. They tend to view questions solely in organizational terms, rather than in larger contextual terms. In fact, having opportunities to do so is sometimes considered a luxury for which they do not have time. However, one dimension of their organizational frameworks that is often implicitly incorporated into discussions of methodology is the "localist" dimension.

The Localist Influence.   Within Hartford's neighborhood organizing apparatus, localism involves several aspects of the groups' functioning. In its most basic manifestation, it often involves characterizing problems as being in large part locally created, but more importantly, amenable to locally produced solutions. Moreover, localism influences organizations to select those issues for action that are more suited to local solutions and to eschew involvement in the more difficult regional or national issues or problems that affect community life. This also fosters an orientation toward very specific geographic areas, and tackling only those issues within the organization's specific turf, sometimes to the detriment of other neighborhoods. For example, when neighborhood groups demand that police deal with prostitution in a given neighborhood (a frequent demand in various areas of Hartford), often the problem is not eliminated but simply displaced into another neighborhood, and the new location may be in another organization's turf.

While this localism helps the neighborhood organizations develop their potential, it may limit the potential of the individual participants. It may also deter individuals from participating in those organizations that do attempt to deal with larger systemic issues.

This localist orientation also helps to explain the reticence on the part of the organizations' staffs to encourage participation in coalitions—such associations take their activists outside the local organizational boundaries and into expanded arenas with different goals and models of organizing. Moreover, building alliances as a means of improving the general climate in which they function is not a goal in and of itself for the neighborhood groups. Rather, as discussed earlier, alliances or coalitions are approached with specific ends in mind, and the localist orientation contributes to this tendency.

A localist orientation may serve, moreover, to diminish or underestimate issues of racism and race relations in general. Biased attitudes verbalized by neighborhood residents or behaviors that reflect bias are dealt with on an ad hoc basis by organizers, sometimes confronted and sometimes ignored. The assumption by organizers is that over time, in the process of working on issues, participants of different racial and ethnic backgrounds will come to recognize their common interests, and racist ideas will gradually subside and eventually wither away. Unless championed by a particular organizer or director—in most cases a person of color—racism is not dealt with as an issue in and of itself, or as an impediment to unity, as many labor organizers characterize it. While all of the full-time staff members sincerely deplore racist ideas and behavior, the model of neighborhood organizing embraced in Hartford does not explicitly factor race or racism into its methodology.

In the case of ONE-CHANE, where the organization's active participants are almost exclusively African American and Puerto Rican, an important challenge is to prevent cleavages between these two groupings rather than dealing with racism on the part of white participants, since there are so few whites in the organization. However, within both AHOP and HART, where there is significant white participation, the issue of racism or instances of racist behavior can impede efforts. None of the organizations would ever absorb an overtly racist group or block club under its umbrella.

Newsletters and Printed Material.   The three organizations do not publish a great quantity or variety of materials, and there is a notable lack of analysis within their various publications. What is distributed to neighborhood residents usually are more detailed accounts of what they might read in the local newspaper. So it is not a strong conceptual or ideological message that gets transmitted into the community from the three organizations, but instead a list of accomplishments and sometimes chronologies of events surrounding a given issue. HART's newsletter, "HART Times," is published several times a year, and many of the articles are written by the neighborhood residents who are involved with particular issues, offering another avenue for participation in the organization.

AHOP's activities are reported in a newsletter, "Asylum Hill Ink," published approximately six times a year by the community organization Asylum Hill, Inc., which collaborates with AHOP on many activities. Asylum Hill, Inc., has existed in the neighborhood since the early 1970s and in many respects has been overshadowed by AHOP, although the two organizations cooperate in different endeavors. Asylum Hill, Inc., receives funding from Aetna Life and Casualty and Connecticut Mutual Insurance for general operation expenses, and funds from the city and state governments for the operation of employment programs. ONE-CHANE has no regular newsletter but periodically mails announcements of different events and mobilizations.

Analysis of problems or issues is presented, not in the printed materials, but rather in the context of the ongoing work in the communities and meetings and planning sessions in which time is set aside for such assessment. So unless one is an active participant in a committee, on the board of one of the groups, or in the various informal communication networks that exist both in the neighborhoods and within the organizations, it is difficult to ascertain their deeper evaluations of the issues.

All three organizations receive substantial coverage in the several weekly and biweekly community newspapers, as well as in Hartford's one major daily newspaper, the *Hartford Courant*. Occasionally the organizations are featured on the community access cable television station in Hartford, although they have not yet made routine use of this outlet.

Neighborhood Issues and Economic Restructuring

Depending on the specific agenda at hand, the issues of collective consumption addressed by the neighborhood organizations may or may not be immediately related to issues of economic restructuring. To the extent that any concern of urban neighborhood residents can be placed within a context of economic development, one could say that the issues of the neighborhood organizations are a consequence of that development, that these organizations confront the local manifestations of national economic trends. So, for example, if the crime and drug problem can be described as derived from a configuration of larger national economic forces in which the lack of opportunity for economic advancement of the poorest segments of society leads to involvement with crime and drugs and, further, that this lack of opportunity is traced in part to the problems of the contemporary segmented urban labor market, then one might argue that there is a relationship, perhaps tenuous, between such issues and economic restructuring.

If one is looking, however, for a closer mapping of neighborhood organizations' issues to specific stages in urban economic development, then it is more difficult to delineate such relationships or demonstrate cause and effect between economic restructuring and an increase in a local problem such as crime. Problems such as crime and drugs may emanate from economic and social inequality, but once unleashed, they take on dynamics of their own.

Many issues addressed by Hartford's neighborhood organizations in the late 1980s and the beginning of the 1990s do not appear to be as directly related to economic restructuring as the issues that were important earlier in the decade. Public outcry over questions such as who reaps the benefits of downtown development diminished by the late 1980s as the pace of development slowed considerably in Hartford, the recession unfolded, and the ambitious plans of developers were interrupted or halted. In fact, in mid 1990, according to one account in the *New York Times,* Hartford's downtown was dying (Johnson 1990). Despite the fact that a local organization, Citizen Research Education Network, conducted a study (1990) that calculated the revenues that linkage would have brought into city coffers had it been adopted, the neighborhood organizations did not embrace the report's findings as the basis of any new linkage campaign. What has consumed much more of the neighborhood organizations' energies are questions of state and local taxation, municipal budgets, resources for education, and as mentioned throughout this chapter, the crime and drug problem, rather than demands for linkage.

There are obvious relationships between the general economic health of the city, the region, and the local tax base and many of the questions faced in the neighborhoods—whether municipal budget shortfalls result from the revenue loss associated with capital flight or failed condominium projects—but the ways in which these issues are perceived, defined, and experienced by neighborhood residents and organizations tend not to highlight such connections. Rather, more recently, issues tend to be addressed as distinct or isolated problems, with less emphasis on corporate power or advantage and more on the practices of the local government.

There are several consequences of the neighborhood organizations' methods of framing issues, especially in terms of cultivating coalitions with labor. Indeed, the same issues facing the neighborhood organizations face labor union members as they experience community life in Hartford and the surrounding region, since union members are obviously residents of local communities, including Hartford. However, most of these problems are not presently within the scope of work undertaken by unions.

Conversely, since neighborhood issues are not immediately derived from specific problems of industrial relations as experienced in workplaces, they do not appear to be problems with origins common to those of labor. Therefore, coalescing with labor, or developing analyses of community issues that emphasize any common roots of neighborhood problems with those of labor unions are not necessarily either obvious conclusions or necessary strategic choices for neighborhood organization activists. In other words, the manner in which neighborhood activists tend to conceptualize and experience their struggles does not necessarily lead them to see or to seek commonalities with union members who experience economic and social insecurity arising from a changing economy. This is one more reason why the building of coalitions and alliances between labor and community organizations is often difficult.

Beyond issues of organizing methods, who participates, and which problems motivate participation, organizational structure and maintenance issues also bear heavily on the potential and accomplishments of the neighborhood organizations. As with labor unions, these factors can either facilitate or impede empowerment.

STRUCTURE AND MAINTENANCE ISSUES

The structural features of the groups characterize their work and influence their effectiveness. Issues of leadership and staffing cycles within the organizations may also be problematic. Beyond these issues, there are spin-off effects and new organizations that are created by the three neighborhood organizations and that demonstrate their viability.

Structures and Processes

All three of the organizations have similar structures: a board of directors, elected at an annual community congress, whose members come from the constituent units or block/area clubs or, in some cases, individual community activists whose membership on the board enhances its capacity. For example, among other constituencies, AHOP's board of directors includes members from churches within the Asylum Hill neighborhood. This arrangement helps to maintain support and involvement by the churches, despite the fact that large percentages of their respective congregations live outside both Asylum Hill and even Hartford.

The boards of directors hire the executive directors, and the executive directors hire other staff members. There are the typical additional sets of officers besides presidents: various vice-presidents, secretaries, treasurers, and so on. The boards meet specified numbers of times each year and consider organizational priorities and the progress of various issue campaigns. As with many community boards, much of their work is quite routine, although there are occasions when controversy arises and dissension results. For example, at one point during the late 1980s, the AHOP board asked one executive director to resign due to his inability to effectively facilitate grassroots organizing.

Through these structures, community residents have formal control over the organizations. The board members represent a range of issues, constituencies, and organized segments in the respective areas of Hartford. However, the bulk of the groups' work takes place in the various issue committees, local block or area committees, and task forces rather than at their boards or in the board meetings.

The annual congress that each organization holds is very important to its functioning. ONE-CHANE and AHOP hold their congresses in the spring, and HART's takes place in the fall. Hundreds of hours of collective work go into planning and organizing these events. The organizing attempts to tap into and mobilize every possible constituency and every single participant from each organization. Staff, leadership, and often UCAN consultants involve themselves in the preparations through various committees. Low-priced tickets are sold (one or two dollars, including dinner) and are distributed by all organizational activists in order to broaden participation and ensure attendance. Program books with advertisements from local businesses and politicians are also produced. Numerous roles and tasks arc assigned to dozens of people so that responsibility and ownership of the event is shared.

The congresses are usually held in a school auditorium or cafeteria and tend to attract several hundred people. Typically the agenda includes introductions of various officers of the organization and moderators for the day's event, reports from planning committees, reports from issue committees on accomplishments during the past year, some type of accountability session with local public officials on one or more current issues, presentation of a slate and election of officers, and votes on organizational priorities. Sometimes issue workshops are held; these may also include discussion or "mini" accountability sessions with public officials. There is often entertainment, featuring performances by youth groups or choirs from the local churches or institutions within the organization's turf.

For organizations who trace their methodologies to Alinsky's confrontational tactics, the gatherings tend to be free from conflict or dissension. Moreover, for organizations who claim to foster participatory decision making, the congresses are so highly orchestrated and the agenda so tightly controlled that few substantive decisions are made. Generally the slate of officers and executive board members that is offered by a nominating committee is uncontested. Challenges or competing slates are rare. These slates are generally quite representative of the different constituencies and groupings within the organizations, so that those who are elected tend to reflect the ranges of activism and viewpoints within the organizations. But the real decision making in this regard is done before the congresses take place.

The accountability sessions are likewise well rehearsed, as is the case with other settings for accountability sessions. Sometimes the congress moderator may even discourage participants from actively confronting public officials on issues of concern in order to maintain control of the session.

These congresses do help to develop a deeper sense of community among the participants, especially a sense of pride in the cumulative yearly achievements of the organizations. The congresses also serve as a reminder to elected and other public officials of the potential power of these groups to present claims to the government and of their power to organize and accomplish their goals. Particularly at HART's congress, which takes place in the peak of the campaign season for local elections in alternate years, office seekers are able to reach several hundred concerned residents and potential voters.

Despite the fact that the format and outcomes of the community congresses vary little from year to year, the organizations continue to sponsor the annual events. For the leadership, particularly the respective staffs, the congress becomes in some measure a test of both their organizing capabilities and the general coherence of the organizations. A great deal of importance is attached to gross attendance figures, and in fact, one of the program evaluation measures submitted to prospective funders is the number of individuals who have attended the various organizational events and mobilizations, the most important of which is the annual congress.

Staffing, Leadership, and Organizational Cycles

One important characteristic of the work of the neighborhood organizations in Hartford is a cyclical effect of their work and leadership. There are definite ebbs and flows of activity within the organizations, especially publicly noticed or reported activity, and this phenomenon can be partially traced to staff and leadership turnover. The turnover is both intentional and unintentional.

Elected neighborhood-based leadership is mandated by the respective bylaws to change at least every two years, that is, a president may serve a maximum of two one-year terms. Often a person serves a single one-year term as president. One of the consequences of this turnover is the problem of what to do with past presidents: These are individuals who usually have undergone intensive training and development to become leaders, to whom the organizations have devoted considerable amounts of resources— particularly in the form of staff attention—and who, at the end of one or two years of concentrated activity and energy, no longer have a very important organizational role to fulfill.

Some past presidents remain on the boards of directors, but eventually most tend to drift away from the organization. Several have gone on to play important roles in the community in other capacities: An AHOP past president, Marie Kirkley-Bey, went on to become active in politics and was elected as one of the first People for Change council members; Ron Cretaro, a former HART president, was the first chairperson of People for Change; and Alta Lash remains closely tied to neighborhood organizing as one of UCAN's two staff members who provide technical assistance to the neighborhood groups and other organizations. Yet these examples tend to be the exceptions. Often by the time five years has elapsed, a person who was once president is no longer active within the organization in any capacity. Organizers acknowledge this as a problem that should be addressed but that somehow never becomes part of any organization's agenda.

The issue can have even more ramifications as it relates to staff and staff turnover. Although by the end of the 1980s the salaries for organizers employed by these three groups were in the mid-twenty-thousand-dollar range, it is a very demanding job in terms of hours, energy, and concentration. It is often difficult to fill vacancies, and individual organizers can suffer burnout if they don't develop pacing and coping mechanisms, or adopt a long-term perspective on the nature of, and potential for, change. The job can easily strain family life.

Beyond these issues, there are various ways in which cooptation away from neighborhood organizing and toward assimilation into the local power structure can occur. Talented organizers become recognized by both their allies and their organizing targets, and the targets generally have enticements of jobs and higher salaries available to offer. Occasionally a past director or organizer has taken a position with an entity such as a for-profit housing development concern. However, many organizers who leave the groups' employ end up in other human service or nonprofit organizations.

What results from this turnover is a cycle of organizational ability and effectiveness. It takes several years for new staff and new leadership to develop the full potential of the confluence of organizational resources that come together at the beginning of any given cycle. Kevin Kelly, AHOP's first director, commented to the *Hartford Courant* (Romash 1987) specifically on this trend: "It's not unusual for community groups to go through cycles. You need to build, maintain, rebuild, maintain." Moreover, once the groups reach a peak of organizational capacity, if the key actors start to remove themselves from the situation, the groups' effectiveness can rapidly diminish.

In the late 1980s this phenomenon occurred in Hartford. All three organizations experienced tremendous staff turnover: Each changed directors at least twice, and organizer turnover was even more pronounced. The directors of the three organizations during the previous several years had achieved a very collaborative relationship and were able to guide the organizations to function in mutually complementary ways. The collective departure of AHOP's Kevin Kelly, HART's Mike Allison, and ONE-CHANE's Eddie Perez over a relatively short time span effected significant changes for each individual organization as well as for their collective functioning. HART seemed to have the most developed organizational infrastructure and the greatest ability to maintain momentum. Its two succeeding executive directors provided a great deal of continuity for the organization. However, AHOP had to totally reconstruct its apparatus and rebuild its organizing capacity with an almost entirely new staff. In the early 1990s, ONE-CHANE is assuming more community development functions and, while still involved in organizing, is balancing these two functions.

Another aspect of the organizational effectiveness cycle involves what one veteran organizer described as a certain type of limit or set of limits to the scope and reach of the organizations. Rick Kozin, who held organizing positions at HART and ONE-CHANE before moving to Nebraska to continue his organizing career, observed that there may come a point when the organizations are at such a peak of activity and effectiveness that the logical next steps involve the groups themselves actually creating the goods or services that they demand (a prime example is housing) or filling the elected positions of municipal government to be able to set more neighborhood-oriented public policy.

In Hartford, given the particular set of constraints in funding and the supporting organizational bylaw provisions that preclude direct sponsorship of partisan political activity, community development has been the more available route. Of course, one of the major stimuli for People for Change came from the failed linkage campaign waged by these neighborhood organizations and specifically from several of their key community leaders, but the organizations as entities could not officially sponsor or participate in People for Change, as discussed earlier in great detail. The neighborhood organizations, therefore, have in several different ways pursued development options as well as other types of social service provision: their "spin-off effects."

Mergers and Spin-offs

The neighborhood groups in Hartford have sometimes absorbed other entities and sometimes created new organizations. Before examining these developments, it is useful to consider the incentives for participation offered by the organizations and to analyze the spin-offs in view of these incentives and how they address the needs that motivate residents' participation in the first place.

Incentives and the Context for Spin-offs. In response to the continuing need in the city of Hartford for affordable housing, all three organizations engage in housing-related activities. Besides helping to create housing development corporations, they provide different forms of information to area residents. HART holds housing fairs where representatives of lending institutions and housing service organizations help first-time home buyers find their way through the maze of programs, processes, and paperwork associated with the purchase of a home. This tame but helpful service helps establish HART's worth to a segment of the population who may not yet want to storm City Hall.

In the area of social service provision, AHOP's unemployment group, the Communication Development Employment Council (CDEC), evolved from direct action and advocacy to a more traditional job-training, readiness, and referral service. AHOP facilitated this shift through its relationship with Asylum Hill, Inc., which administered a state-assisted job-training program. AHOP's ability to refer interested individuals to the program is also an incentive for involvement with the organization. In the early 1990s HART began to seek and receive municipal and private grants for social services to youth in its neighborhood who have been arrested and also for antidrug education activities, affording it both new funding sources and new areas of program development for an important constituency.

These services enhance the intellectual and political appeal of the concept of community empowerment by stimulating interest and participation in the organizations. Yet there is still the question of grassroots organizing as the definitive feature of the organizations. The balance between development activities and organizing may shift, but organizing will likely remain prominent in all three groups.

Mergers.   Two of the Hartford neighborhood groups in their current form represent combinations of previously separate organizations. ONE-CHANE resulted from the merger of the neighborhood association ONE, whose programs included development and social services, with the more neo-Alinsky-oriented CHANE. However, CHANE also undertook housing development projects prior to the 1988 merger, as a constituency interested in development activities existed within the group throughout its early history.

AHOP has a rather complex set of relationships with other organizations. In its early years it absorbed an independent social service organization in Asylum Hill, the Hill Center, and now continues to provide a number of social services once provided by this center, but with a distinctive grassroots organizing flavor. The building that once housed the Hill Center now houses AHOP. Asylum Hill, Inc. (AHI), mentioned earlier, collaborates with AHOP on employment programs and other activities such as a newsletter. AHI together with the Hill Center and five area churches constituted AHOP's initial sponsoring organizations in the early 1980s.

Spin-offs.   In response to the pressing need to acquire local apartment buildings in order to maintain them as affordable units, AHOP created a housing development organization, Hill Housing, Inc. Hill Housing is in many respects a subsidiary of AHOP, and AHOP's first director became Hill Housing's first director.

Besides this direct spin-off, AHOP helped to create a local child care center in cooperation with a local church and the Hartford Region YWCA, whose main branch is located in Asylum Hill. AHOP also maintains a cooperative relationship with a local soup kitchen, Loaves and Fishes, shares information and referral resources, and jointly coordinates a small emergency relief fund with the kitchen. Finally, in the early 1990s, AHOP had plans to develop a new, larger community center that could accommodate a broader range of activities in Asylum Hill than is currently possible in AHOP's present building or in combination with other organizations and the local churches.

HART was one of the organizations who were instrumental in creating the Broad-Park Development Corporation. Although it works with dozens of organizations throughout the southern part of Hartford as necessary, HART itself has been less actively involved in facilitating new local organizations than has AHOP. Rather, HART has sought to diversify its own funding base and ventured into various social service activities.

These patterns indicate that neighborhood organizing in Hartford is partially built upon other local neighborhood organizations and can be instrumental in creating new community-based institutions. The spin-off effects manifest themselves not merely as other organizations, but also as new social processes in the neighborhoods and the city.

CONCLUSIONS

It is difficult to imagine the social and political landscape of Hartford without the neo-Alinsky neighborhood organizations. The concerns of the residents and the issues that these groups address would still exist and give rise to some form of organization. What is interesting in Hartford is the particular pattern of grassroots organization that has evolved through the presence of AHOP, HART, and ONE-CHANE.

Clearly these organizations have provided opportunities for popular participation in local developments and avenues for popular expression. Their activities help to demystify government processes and social issues for neighborhood residents. They have been able to protect residents from certain aspects of the deterioration of urban life and communities as experienced in older Northeast cities. However, that process of deterioration continues to erode the social fabric of Hartford and other major cities in the early nineties.

In the face of overwhelming poverty and the dire needs of the population, the efforts of the neighborhood organizations may resemble someone plugging a leak in a dam with one finger, only to have a new leak spring up elsewhere. The constraints of both methodology and insufficient power or resources tend to compound the difficulties in addressing local problems.

Methodologically, the localist orientation fosters a propensity to address all issues that arise in a particular area. The concerns of AHOP and ONE-CHANE are moving in a redistributive direction, with goals of social equality and a continuing strong role for local government in solving social problems. However, in HART's larger geographical area, many influences move in conflicting and sometimes outright contradictory directions, placing HART as an organization in the position of mediating conflicting sets of demands. HART's significant constituencies of older homeowners and small-business people (many of whom live outside Hartford and operate businesses or own property in the city) make demands for lower taxes and reductions in municipal spending which come into conflict with other constituencies' demands for greater levels of service, especially in the areas of education and public safety. This is a delicate situation for the organization, both with respect to internal coherence and external relationships with other community organizations. Moreover, adding to the complexities, the issue of race relations is always under the surface but tends to be minimized by the organizations.

Victories for neighborhood organizations are very hard fought in many instances, especially those involving landlords or the local bureaucracy. Often success must be measured in small doses, in very incremental units, or in a group's capacity to prevent further erosion of the quality of life in an area. They are often successful in forcing powerful interests to pay attention to their presence and demands, but they may not always possess the power to significantly alter the overall direction of development in a given neighborhood. Nonetheless, through the years they have become adept at working through the maze of zoning boards and city departments to attempt to forestall some plans. However, when these groups do manage to create their own institutions, housing development corporations, or day care centers, they experience a deeper sense of organizational accomplishment and power.

By building upon other local institutions such as churches, small service organizations, or neighborhood improvement associations, these neighborhood organizations have attained a measure of power for neighborhood residents. Yet, that power is rather elusive and fluctuates with the cycles of organizational effectiveness. Individual leadership plays a significant role in each organization, yet the cyclical effect of changing leadership makes for a measure of discontinuity, as well. Still, in Hartford's mix of conflicting and competing interests, these groups do command accountability.

There are times when the work of the neighborhood groups has a great deal in common with that of labor, but this is often not the case. The common roots of problems experienced by both labor and neighborhood organizations are not necessarily apparent, and alliances with labor are not automatically sought by the neighborhood groups.

Concluding Thoughts

One of the basic differences between unions and neighborhood groups lies in their organizational structures. Neighborhood organizations are made up of volunteers who can come and go, and the organizations are constituted to accommodate these conditions. Unions consist of dues-paying members who, in rare cases, can sue the organization if they feel their interests have not been properly represented, in much the same way the client of an attorney or physician can sue for malpractice. In effect, unions have a legal accountability to their members. Inasmuch as the neighborhood organizations are nonprofit corporations, they are accountable to contributors and boards of directors, but their accountability to the people who participate in their activities is less formal.

All of the organizations attempt to increase their numbers and expand their influence. The tendency toward larger amalgamated organizations exists in all three Hartford area unions, as well as in patterns of mergers with other locals or international unions. Larger organizations afford more power and leverage, both with employers and in the political arena. The neighborhood groups enlarge the scope of their work in two ways: by initiating more constituency groups, block clubs, and other activities, and by diversifying their functions through forming social service organizations, assuming housing development responsibilities, or creating spin-offs. So while unions increase their power by new organizing and joining with other unions, neighborhood groups, who can't determine their membership based on the number of people who pay dues, increase their power by developing their role in the community and sometimes by absorbing other smaller organizations.

One striking difference in the processes of the two types of organizations is found in the role of the organizer. The role of the labor organizer in dealing with members or potential members is directive; that is, the organizer conducts the meetings and has clear responsibility for its direction. Labor organizers fulfill their roles by constructing agendas for meetings and assigning tasks to be undertaken. Rank-and-file members may sometimes run meetings on their own, but the organizer is in essence a link to the rest of the union.

Within the meetings of neighborhood organizations, the organizers play a more facilitating, consultative, and less directive role. Neighborhood residents or one of the group participants conduct the meetings, and the organizer tends to inject himself or herself only at critical moments in order to clarify a situation or set of options, or to suggest something that may be overlooked by others in attendance.

In both types of organizations, however, the organizer does not perform tasks required to advance the organization but rather facilitates the members and participants in assuming responsibilities and accepting assignments. Both kinds of organizers look for similar qualities in potential leaders, particularly the willingness to accept the organization's goals and to take responsibility for the process of empowerment.

For unions, there has been a fairly large distinction between what is required in organizing new members and much of the rest of their work. Work with existing memberships is similar to new organizing in terms of the goal of getting members to take on responsibilities and learn how to organize themselves. Yet, most of the work with organized worksites involves different, often very complex issues and problems. After the struggle to get the union's "foot in the door" is over, staying in the room is difficult and must be negotiated and renegotiated. In an era of overt union busting, staying organized is coming to resemble new organizing in terms of what may be required of members. In some instances it is more difficult: The four-year-long strike at Colt was more challenging to sustain than are most union organizing drives.

All of this is said to contrast the challenges inherent in different phases of unions' work with that of neighborhood organizing, where such ready demarcations do not exist. Rather, work with the participants in neighborhood organizations consists more of a developmental process in which, over time, participants strengthen their capacity to take on increasingly more difficult issues. However, there is greater latitude for the neighborhood group participants to set their own goals and agenda than for union members, who cannot necessarily anticipate, and certainly cannot control, what employers might do. Moreover, unionized work sites can be decertified: The workers can vote to do away with their union and unionized status. For a neighborhood organization, participation in a given area may dwindle, but residents do not have the option of formally voting the organization out of existence.

While there is an observable cyclical effect of organizational capacity and leadership effectiveness within the neighborhood organizations, there is not an analogous process observed among the labor unions. Perhaps because the tenure among many of the leaders of these particular unions has been quite lengthy, and the fact that union offices involve full-time employment with consequently more incentive for individuals to remain in the position, the same type of effect could not be observed.

The labor unions have a rich and varied history to inform and guide their work. Each of the three unions situates its work within either its own traditions or this more general history. For the neighborhood organizations there is not an analogous history or tradition to which participants and leadership relate, save the localized tradition within Hartford over the span of years of the three organizations' existence and a very general reference to Alinsky. Although the various national organizations and networks described earlier are beginning to define a history of neighborhood organizing, and scholar-activists such as Fisher (1984) and Delgado (1986) are beginning to analyze its effects, the Hartford organizations tend not to relate to these national developments or situate themselves within a larger national history or tradition. However, one might argue that the Hartford groups broadly incorporate New Left models of participatory-democratic organizational style, combined with elements from the Catholic left, of which the founders of HART were a part.

Both organizational styles carry the potential for manipulation of membership by leaders, but both have various checks and balances. Both also offer a variety of opportunities for participation by grassroots people or rank-and-file members. Each confronts power with different kinds of strategies and tactics.

CONFRONTING AND WIELDING POWER

For unions, issues and goals have tended to be quite specific: winning a collective-bargaining election, winning a particular grievance, negotiating a contract, and so on. These work-site issues became more difficult to win during the increasingly hostile climate of the 1980s. Much of the labor movement was ill-prepared for the task, having become accustomed to the legitimacy afforded labor in the post–World War II era.

The neighborhood organizations were born, or grew to maturity, in this national context of political conservatism and decreasing federal commitment to the welfare state and to urban concerns. Their methods were formulated within this climate and designed not to rely on legal structures for legitimacy. Hartford neighborhood organizations built themselves almost from scratch, with assistance from local religious organizations, and largely apart from other social movements. Neighborhood organizations, like unions, concerned themselves with very specific issues, but not at any real cost organizationally: Neighborhood organizations have not been the target of the same type of assault as have unions and have not had to be as introspective about how to confront a hostile external climate.

Strategy decisions by all of these groups reflect the desire to win an issue or a struggle. But definitions of success vary, as do what are perceived as obstacles to success. A shop-floor grievance or the installation of a new traffic light involves a fairly specific target and a relatively small group of people to fight for action on the complaint.

In more complex situations, the definition of success may be crucial. For example, although the union eventually won in the Colt strike, questions were often raised during the strike and even in the euphoria following the settlement about whether the victory was worth the costs, especially in human terms. Union members outside the UAW, as well as parties outside the labor movement, voiced this concern. For the UAW, success in the Colt strike was defined and realized in stages. The first stage focused on winning the case at the NLRB. Then came preparation for the eventual back pay award, participation in the buyout, and the strikers' return to work. Success at each stage did not guarantee success at the next, and victory had to be eked out of an incredibly arduous process. Given the tenuous financial position of the new company, the long-term success of the strike is still an open question.

In contrast, 1199 has made decisions to fold strikes in various situations based on what its leadership perceived as the cost in terms of union resources, the potential for success, and the capacity of strikers to persevere. The unions are now fashioning organizing models that allow them to cut their losses and not become mired in losing battles.

Neighborhood organizing, drawing heavily on Alinsky's ideas, readily emphasizes "winnable" struggles and immediate, specific results in order to demonstrate the worth of organizing and to maintain interest and participation in the organizations. The leaders of these organizations want to point to very specific results as proof of their group's viability. Complex issues such as linkage are far more difficult to win, and since the linkage defeat of 1986, the neighborhood groups have become more circumspect about all-or-nothing battles. As difficult as issues such as housing or crime may be, incremental successes may be achieved and claimed as victories by the organizations.

A feature common to both types of organizing is that most successes are built upon mobilizations of members or participants. Both types of organizations also strike a balance between confrontation and compromise, not choosing confrontation in every instance, yet possessing the threat to produce large, boisterous, and disruptive crowds, when necessary. Success is defined not only in terms of winning issues or campaigns, but also as building the capacity of the particular organization in question. Hence 1199 may be willing to see a nursing home close during a strike rather than agree to concessions that would undermine its power against other nursing homes in the future. Likewise, AHOP leaders and staff would rather not have the Guardian Angels enter their turf on the crime issues and, in so doing, undermine group consensus within AHOP because of the surrounding controversy and also create an alternative organization in Asylum Hill. They describe this phenomenon as not being "organizational," meaning that it does not build organizational capacity for AHOP.

Labor organizers emphasize that employers hold immense power over workers by virtue of controlling livelihood and incomes, something they contend is not involved in community or neighborhood organizing. One comparison they might entertain is that of landlords' power over tenants or financial institutions' power over people who face the loss of their homes. But since the major focus of unions' work is on workplace issues that are directly related to the maintenance of people's livelihoods and incomes, there is always great potential to evoke the enmity and wrath of employers and often serious risks for union members who are outspoken. In most neighborhood organizing scenarios, there is not an analogous risk factor.

Building power among union workers necessarily requires building the confidence among workers to confront their employer. Therefore, specific victories over relatively small issues are important in union work as well as in neighborhood organizing. However, it is difficult to remain at this more simplified level of confrontation because eventually contract negotiations arise and the intensity of conflict elevates substantially. Neighborhood organizations have more choice as to how and when to escalate a struggle and may choose not to engage participants in heightened confrontation if they are at a disadvantage. However, this may lead to a perception of the organizations as weak or bluffing.

Perhaps the most important set of differences between the two types of organizations in terms of using and confronting power is in the interaction with laws and legal procedures. The experiences from the Colt strike highlighted how these differences impacted the functioning of the Community-Labor Alliance and the frustrations experienced by neighborhood organizers in conforming with the UAW's reliance on attorneys.

Beyond the use of legal strategies to win strikes, another dimension of this difference may be understood in considering how unions relate to legal and legislative reform: In 1990, for example, unions began lobbying the U.S. Congress for legislation that would outlaw the hiring of permanent replacement workers during strikes—an attempt to enact a law to overcome a disadvantage unions currently suffer. This type of goal, the passage of national legislation, is something that could deeply affect all three Hartford unions analyzed here. However, this type of activity is far beyond the scope of the neighborhood organizations, both in terms of how they view their mission and in what they would commit themselves to accomplishing. Yet, the reforms that unions most require are generally national in scope: They are part of a set of national conditions that are played out in local settings (see Clark 1989). The inherent localism of neighborhood groups' operations and the issues they embrace make them loathe to take on such campaigns.

Neighborhood organizations are more able to take advantage of public-relations-oriented strategies, creating impressions through the media and using tactics like protest to gain leverage. Institutions, banks, or individual public officials are generally very concerned any about negative publicity that neighborhood groups can generate. Unions also use these tactics, but they may not produce results as readily for labor as for neighborhood groups. Colt or other employers may be content to live with bad publicity in order to break their employees' unions. This is another reason why unions pursue legal strategies and legislative reform.

INCENTIVES AND OUTCOMES

People join and participate in both types of organizations for a number of reasons. In the case of unions there are definite material issues that serve as incentives to organize: low pay, poor working conditions, unfair supervisors, lack of benefits, and so on. However, union organizers cite another motivation of a less tangible nature: the desire to be treated with dignity. Not only in the case of the low-paid service workers targeted by 1199 and HERE in organizing drives, but also among the UAW's existing membership and in its new organizing, the quest for dignity on the job is a very crucial factor. In fact, 1199 uses the slogan "Work With Dignity" on buttons, posters, and in other printed materials.

In nursing home organizing, motivation often comes from the owner—perhaps a young white male entrepreneur—who may treat grown women workers more than twice his age, many of whom are African American, West Indian, or Latina, as if they are children incapable of exercising independent judgment or making decisions. The same may be true of hotel managers and even university administrations, as the UAW has discovered with its members who are maintenance workers in institutions of higher education. Organizers maintain that the desire to be treated with respect and dignity on the job is the single most powerful factor in union organizing.

Similar to neighborhood organizing, much of the motivation to unionize emanates from immediate self-interest, although self-interest arising from work site issues. In settings that have been unionized for some time the fervor that sustains new organizing may not be present in the work force, but the need for an ongoing organization to defend employees' interests is generally evident to that segment of the work force who participates in and sustains the organization. Although there is always the potential for antagonism between workers and their supervisors or employers, many workers do not relate actively to their union until some type of crisis erupts or a contract has to be negotiated. The three unions observed here attempt to deal with these classic "free-rider" issues by providing opportunities for involvement by their membership in a wide range of activities from political action to union training sessions to conventions and even charity walkathons.

By creating avenues for involvement in both work site and larger community issues, as these unions attempt to do, they are also diversifying the benefits of membership. While many labor unions are experimenting with membership benefits such as low-interest credit cards, prepaid legal services, low-cost insurance, and other consumer services, these three unions focus less on what some of their leaders consider gimmicks and more on the difficult challenges of organizing and meeting existing members' needs.

Neighborhood organizations build participation upon the self-interest that manifests itself in community problems and issues. Because these issues can sometimes be less obvious or easier to ignore than work site issues, participation in the groups' campaigns may have to be cultivated more deliberately. Since no vote is required to establish the organization, lack of involvement rather than pro or con sentiments may be the problem. A small group of people may raise an issue initially, but a wider audience generally has to be developed and activated in order to sustain an issue campaign. Different incentives may need to be offered to acquaint neighborhood residents with the benefits of participation. Social service provision and housing development are among the incentives and benefits offered by such groups.

However, like the union members' quest for dignity on the job, many individuals are motivated to participate in neighborhood organizations because the groups offer an opportunity to defend the community against speculators, crime, and government excess or transgression. Community empowerment themes do have appeal. Even though the organizations eschew electoral politics, they function as quasi-political entities by aggregating and presenting claims upon the government and, in particular, the local state.

In brief, then, incentives for joining and participating in both the unions and neighborhood organizations have two bases: tangible, material benefits, and issues of individual and collective empowerment. The outcomes of both types of organizational agendas reflect these same two tendencies.

The outcomes of the labor movement's activities are so numerous and complex that it is ludicrous to attempt to proffer a generalized list. Labor history offers myriad insights into a more generalized understanding of history; labor relations influence many social processes well beyond the workplace. However, the three unions of this project have made important specific impacts in Hartford and particularly in the movements for social change in the area.

Out of the Colt strike experience a new awareness has emerged among many local forces of the impact of labor relations on the community at large. The strike generated mutual interest between the labor movement and the neighborhood organizations never previously evidenced. In particular, the eventual outcome of the strikers' regaining their jobs demonstrated the power of unions to community members who had never before paid attention to labor issues.

There are trade unionists who believe that a strike of such duration tends to dampen enthusiasm for new organizing and can have an overall negative effect for union efforts in the area in contract negotiations as well as in organizing. Quantifying this assertion is quite difficult: How does one measure something that did not occur because of the strike against those events that actually did occur? However, it should be noted that it was in the midst of the strike that University of Hartford maintenance workers approached the UAW to organize. The UAW leadership asserts that the maintenance workers' interest in organizing developed because the Colt strikers and the union served as examples of workers' defending themselves.

Effective union techniques serve as examples in arenas other than the workplace. People for Change and LEAP are important examples of the impact that unions, working with other forces and sharing resources, can have in a community, and through the efforts of the UAW and others, these patterns of involvement are being replicated elsewhere.

These effects must be seen against the tremendous obstacles that unions face, both in Hartford and nationally, and the often negative public perception of unions. Setbacks for the labor movement are very public affairs in both the local and national context. For example, when the UAW lost a major organizing drive at Nissan in 1989 in Smyrna, Tennessee, it was highly publicized in every major national media outlet. Little was mentioned about the company's hiring procedures in which workers who would potentially support unionization were systematically screened out of the applicant pool. However, when the UAW won elections at Mack Truck in South Carolina in 1988, or at Freightliner, a subsidiary of the German firm Daimler-Benz, in 1990 in North Carolina, publicity occurred within labor and left publications, but hardly anywhere else. Locally, the closing of two downtown hotels in Hartford has been attributed in some accounts to labor costs that derive from unionization. These events and the media coverage surrounding them can lead to perceptions that unions are no longer necessary or relevant, or that they are such risky propositions that organizing is not worth the gamble and that unions eventually put firms out of business, anyway.

Union leaders and organizers face all of these issues when they approach a new group of workers in the beginning of a campaign or when they start a new round of contract negotiations. Their role in interpreting events and trends to members and potential members is critical in producing the next set of events that will impact the workplace and the community. The union internal education activities and union-produced media are therefore very important in shaping responses among rank-and-file members who can communicate ideas to wider segments of the community and who also may need philosophical or ideological strengthening in preparation for their own struggles.

Whereas the outcomes and effects of the unions' work have implications beyond the confines of the specific work site—wage patterns or legal precedents may be established through certain local developments that influence the prospects for other unions in other areas—the outcomes and effects of the neighborhood organizations' work tend to be more localized in nature and can often be readily demonstrated. Their leadership and participants point to very specific effects: physical changes in neighborhoods, housing rehabilitation in particular buildings, or specific policies adopted by the city government. In neighborhood organizing there is not the constant fear of losing financial and material resources among participants that can inhibit organizing as is the case in labor organizing. The major obstacle is inaction, as opposed to the fear inherent in labor organizing, and the challenge for neighborhood organizers is to engage people and overcome apathy.

Hartford's neighborhood organizations have helped to cultivate and develop new local leadership. As organizations, the three groups face the challenge of maintaining the involvement of past presidents and other former leaders, yet this problem does not diminish the fact that a large number of individuals from the grass roots have learned how to make government and other institutions more responsive to community needs and have gone on to participate in other areas of community life. Not every past president becomes a city council member or the chairperson of a group such as People for Change, but neighborhood organizing has been the springboard for the emergence of many community leaders.

The capacity of the neighborhood organizations to safeguard neighborhood interests is very important for city residents. Developers and city officials must contend with the responses of these organizations. Neighborhood groups, however, face difficulties when questions of municipal services arise and different constituencies within the same organization offer competing sets of demands.

The neighborhood organizations' work is often seen and felt locally, specifically, and concretely. The labor unions' work is not necessarily experienced so visibly, except perhaps during strikes and in the large public events that accompany the strikes or other occasional issues. What this points to is an asymmetry in attempting to compare the two types of organizing. There is not a neat line that divides social life down the middle, with the world of work on one side and life in the community on the other. So while both types of organizing produce beneficial results for members and participants, they are not necessarily analogous in many respects. For example, the phenomenon of union busting is a part of contemporary labor relations, but there is really no equivalent in neighborhood organizing. The relative freedom to operate enjoyed by neighborhood organizations means that they rely on techniques different from those of labor unions, even though there may be some similarities. What both do offer is the opportunity and the training to defend oneself and one's coworkers or neighbors, as well as the potential for individual and collective advancement.

OPPORTUNITIES FOR COLLABORATION

To what degree can the labor unions and neighborhood organizations work together? Except for the electoral area, differences in structure and organizational practices or traditions do not constitute insurmountable barriers. Rather, it is really a question of how open the leaders of the respective organizations are to forging alliances and how tolerant they are of alternative methodologies and ideologies.

Various actors in Hartford differ on this issue. Kip Lockhart, the president of the Greater Hartford Labor Council, and the leadership of UAW Region 9A feel that coalitions are critical to the future of the labor movement, and they factor coalition work into their respective organizations' agendas. Different elements of 1199–New

England and HERE 217 leadership place varying emphasis on coalitions' importance. The neighborhood organizations are even less inclined to enter coalitions unless the purposes coincide unambiguously with organizational goals.

In order for the two types of organizations to collaborate, there needs to be a clear mutual understanding of the respective organizational processes each group adheres to in order to avoid misunderstandings and unrealistic expectations. The groups cannot be pushed to take actions in specific situations for which they do not have adequate preparation. The organizational differences must be respected, even if they seem nonsensical to the respective "outsiders."

By participating in each other's mobilizations, the organizations can build mutual respect and empathy. When HART leaders, for example, can witness 1199's vocalism and militancy, or when HERE's members can support AHOP's tenants groups, common bonds are established. In Hartford, these simple acts of attending other organizations' activities are very difficult to effect: Inertia can result from inflexibility in individuals' schedules, lack of sufficient mutual interest, or not elevating the support of other groups' activities to a priority.

In Hartford, it could be important to their own effectiveness for organizations to work together, if for no other reason than the fact that neither type of organization on its own can address all the issues. For example, low-paid workers in insecure employment also are likely to inhabit the worst housing in a city, and the problems in both arenas can compound and reinforce each other. At this stage, it is unlikely that the unions in Hartford are going to devote huge amounts of energy to housing-related issues, even though the union leadership may recognize their importance.

Health care accessibility and affordability is another area in which it would make sense for both types of organizations to collaborate, given that many recent strikes have focused in large measure on who will bear the burden of health care coverage, and the most pressing concern for all of the neighborhood organizations' seniors groups is health care costs. Fledgling efforts at coalitions on health care have been attempted in Hartford, but there is room for much more collaboration. Employment creation would also seem a natural point of mutual concern, but only minimal joint efforts have ever been undertaken. These areas could be the first steps in assembling an equity agenda that of necessity would later tackle other issues of inequality, particularly those raised in the *Sheff v. O'Neill* suit. Yet, progress in developing mutual agendas comes slowly, with both groups having to overcome mistrust and reticence at sharing resources, human and otherwise, especially on the part of the neighborhood organizations.

From Hartford's experiences with coalitions, it seems that at this point labor unions have a more apparent need for cooperation from the neighborhood organizations in such matters as strike support or occasionally in organizing drives, yet there are less obvious ways in which neighborhood organizations could benefit from labor union support. For example, in the fall of 1990, as a result of an emphasis on education-related issues within their work, a school bond referendum on the November ballot became a priority for both HART and AHOP. Their lack of previous organizational involvement with electoral campaigns led them to overlook several steps that would have made their task easier (such as adhering to established deadlines to make endorsements), but they did make a general request to the labor movement to support the bond questions. Much more cooperation might have been achieved, especially since the unions participate routinely in electoral work.

CROSSING THE BOUNDARY OF WORK AND COMMUNITY

One of the key questions I explore in this book is how labor organizing and neighborhood organizing inform each other across the boundary of work and community, and how they complement each other.

The greatest similarities seem to be in how both forms of

organizing identify and cultivate leadership, engage frustration and anger to serve meaningful purposes, and attempt to confront and redefine power relationships in their respective environments. The dissimilarities in organizational structures, relationships to legal processes, and ability to control agendas and timing with respect to issues or campaigns differentiate the organizations. Moreover, within labor organizing, ideology—including leftist ideology—can be an important tool. If a union chooses, there is space for ideology within their methodology: Both 1199 and HERE 217 exhibit an ideological approach to their work. Within neighborhood organizing, in Hartford and elsewhere, no space has been created for explicitly ideological approaches to the work, much to the concern of analysts such as Fisher (1984) and Delgado (1986). There is also the issue of partisan electoral work—one of the greatest barriers to collaboration—as well as the very different funding bases and very different types of accountability. Given all of this, where might the two types of organizing inform each other?

Their respective histories suggest that they do not explicitly inform each other, except within the references to Alinsky's original vision and his inspiration for neighborhood organizing from labor and the CIO. There is little evidence that mutual interest ever leads to attempts to learn from each other, though there could be fruitful exchanges in areas where targets and strategies and tactics are most different.

Both types of groups could benefit from an understanding of the other's practices. Labor could benefit from a greater appreciation of, or new tactics for, operating outside externally imposed legal constraints. Neighborhood organizing could benefit from learning how, without surrendering autonomy, to use legal options more effectively to achieve their ends and to use legislative reforms to forge social change. Such exchange could certainly be accommodated within the neo-Alinksy vision and could easily be incorporated into labor's thrust toward greater outreach.

If it is more appropriate to suggest that the two styles of organizing complement each other, I must emphasize that there are also many more examples of social movements than either the sum of these two types of organizations' activities or their separate enterprises represent. So if they complement each other, they also complement other movements as well, and vice versa. Certainly in Hartford, civil rights and issues of race relations are extremely salient for residents. The questions of race and equity posed in the *Sheff v. O'Neill* desegregation lawsuit are some of the most important issues faced by the city, indeed the entire state, and will confront both Hartford's unions and neighborhood organizations in years to come. Moreover, there is not a symmetry between labor and neighborhood organizing: They are not necessarily equal or equivalent in terms of processes or outcomes, and the two parts do not add up to one whole, but rather only a fraction of the large spectrum of social movements. Yet, several ways in which these two movements complement each other should be considered.

First, both focus on quality-of-life issues in their respective environments and on material outcomes. Income, employment, housing, public service provision, and their various other concerns all combine to affect standards of living in given communities, in this case Hartford. The impacts of both labor and neighborhood organizing do result in specific consequences for the community and help define social life in the community. Second, the ways in which individuals learn to confront their conditions—their landlord or employer or elected official—also impact the quality of life, but in a less tangible fashion. With varying degrees of success, these two types of organizations offer people hope that they can change conditions, that their efforts and collective can become factors in power equations. The notion of empowerment—a process of people's gaining control over their lives—remains a powerful motivation, and the work of both types of organizations offers genuine avenues to achieve degrees of empowerment.

Empowerment may need to be understood as meaning different things in each sphere, experienced in quite different ways and evaluated using distinct criteria. Accordingly, each form of organizing takes a very dissimilar road toward a goal that each conceives of as empowerment. Moreover, empowerment may also need to be understood as much as a process or condition to be attained as it is an outcome: more input into the course of community development, less intimidation in the workplace—each of which is very qualitative, involving both the "what" and the "how" in its respective organizing arena.

The different meanings and outcomes that empowerment embodies may flow from both the different logics of the organizing in the two arenas and the different social dynamics that give rise to organizing in each sphere. For specific individuals, problems in one or the other—the workplace or the community—may be more compelling. However, workplace relations and conditions in neighborhoods and communities in combination with other factors produce the living standards and the possibilities of improving life for individuals, families, and the larger community. The social processes that create troubled environments in either sphere may or may not be closely related, but the resulting conditions constitute what is experienced in a community. In this sense the achievements of the two types of organizing come to complement each other and impact the social fabric of a city.

CONFRONTING ECONOMIC RESTRUCTURING

The experiences in coalitions, and the new methods of labor organizing and neighborhood organizing illustrate the variety of ways in which the organizations deal with economic restructuring. Certain methodologies are examples of refining techniques to meet more extreme conditions, for example, the Blitz model of labor organizing. Other activities create new forms of community-controlled services and development: AHOP's spawning of Hill Housing, Inc., or HART's housing fairs. However, there are other activities that present new demands and new claims on government and begin to redefine the public agenda.

The Community-Labor Alliance transformed the Colt strike into a public issue and forced public officials to take positions on the issue, recasting the strike from the status of a "private" matter between employer and employees to a communitywide issue with communitywide implications. People for Change attempts to take this further by pressing for new types of local government action and intervention that support the needs of union members, neighborhood residents and their organizations, and also the demands of civil rights, women's, gay rights, homeless advocacy organizations, and others. Although labor has historically been active in the political arena, People for Change attempts to sharpen the involvement and redefine the way issues are articulated and addressed. During its first four years it enjoyed modest victories in terms of winning votes within city council deliberations, yet it has been able to recast political debate in Hartford.

Certain features of the organizations' work in this economic context can be described perhaps as inevitable; that is, a union would be expected to fight a plant closing or negotiate for wage increases and improved working conditions. In that sense, the question arises as to what is new about their responses in this time period versus the pre-1970s onset of restructuring. Based on the Hartford experiences, I would argue that one of the most important factors has to be the ability of labor leadership to understand emerging trends, assess situations, and forge new courses of action, albeit risky ones. The innovations in Hartford are in large part due to this capacity in the union leadership.

In the case of the neighborhood organizations, their entire, relatively brief histories have been built by clearing new paths and cultivating new grassroots leadership. The choices that the organizational leadership—professional staff, consultants, and neighborhood residents—have made also flow from the combination of their methods, analytical abilities, and visions for their respective communities. There has been nothing inevitable in their work, it has been based on their judgment and choices: They have defined their own courses of action, with varying results.

As the 1990s unfold, the simmering combination of issues of race relations and inequality and the unabating process of economic restructuring in cities such as Hartford produce urban social conditions that are almost beyond crisis stage. Explosions like those in Los Angeles in 1992 are the nightmares of leaders of all large American cities. These realities challenge all organizations engaged in social change.

In Hartford, the neighborhood groups seem to possess neither the organizational capacity nor the vision to intervene effectively and alter the larger contours of social development that lead to the drastic inequality endured in the city. The unions are consumed in struggles for their own viability or survival, despite the 1992 presidential election. Neither type of organization seems capable of tackling many of the larger questions of social equity. Their own victories or breakthroughs take place on an occasional basis, and it is not possible for them to count on a consistent pattern of success from which to build a larger social agenda. Yet their work is still worth examining, even if it only chips away at inequity a bit at a time. It signifies the origins from which larger social movements may emerge, or the limited type of social change with which we may need to be satisfied for some period of time. Since no grandiose solutions to the problems of inequality in Hartford are on anyone's drawing board, the process of change will likely be slow, tedious, and undramatic. Any innovations or successes in the area of social change will provide useful insights for the future.

CONDITIONS IN HARTFORD COMPARED TO THOSE ELSEWHERE

The strike support coalitions and community-labor alliances that emerged specifically in Hartford conform with patterns elsewhere, from the Pittston strike by the United Mine Workers to the Jay, Maine, paperworkers' strike (see Brecher and Costello 1990, and my account of Hartford in Simmons 1990). Issues once thought to be labor's province—strikes, capital flight, and others—are now often understood as problems affecting entire communities.

Electoral coalitions are also demonstrative of Brecher and Costello's "emerging alliance" of labor and community forces, and People for Change (PFC) and LEAP are indeed being examined in other locales: PFC activists have been called upon to share their experiences at forums in Boston, Cambridge, and Philadelphia. LEAP's first executive director helped to establish similar statewide coalitions in New England, including the Commonwealth Coalition in Massachusetts, the Granite State Coalition in New Hampshire, the Ocean State Action in Rhode Island, and the Dirigo Alliance in Maine. These coalitions are in contact with similar formations around the country.

The governmental framework in which People for Change emerged is unique to Hartford and may not be replicable elsewhere. That it arose as a possibility is largely a product of several specific structural features of Hartford's municipal government: the at-large city council elections, the size of the city council at nine members, and the Connecticut statute that mandates minority party representation. Other factors that gave rise to PFC are perhaps found more readily in other cities: disaffected Democrats, labor activists, frustrated community forces, and underrepresented communities of color and other constituencies. Moreover, the option of creating a third party was viewed differently by the various forces involved, some seeing it as goal worthy of a more permanent status and others seeing it a tactical decision for the specific situation. The third-party option may or may not be seen as necessary or possible in other municipalities.

Regional economic differences and specific dominant industries both shape and influence responses of popular forces in other cities. Elsewhere there may be unique local traditions and different perceptions of unions by community forces. So, for example, if labor has been more involved with community issues and local politics than in Hartford, then perhaps the problems encountered both in the CLA and PFC need not emerge. The paperworkers and the Mine Workers each had a different configuration of organizations and forces to work with in their strikes. ACORN has a view of unions different from that of HART, AHOP, or ONE-CHANE.

Many of my examples were drawn from the experience of the Colt strike. This strike was unique, especially in its conclusion. But if it was unique, it had regional and even national implications. First, the work of the CLA would have been important whether the strike was won or lost. Given that the union was able to persevere and win, the CLA's efforts have been hailed as exemplary on a national basis by the UAW and other labor organizations. The determination of the strikers has likewise been hailed nationally. However, there have been other strikes of both larger and smaller proportions that have not resulted in the ultimate success of a union victory, but that have involved the same degree of sacrifice and community solidarity. Labor and community forces can look to these experiences for lessons, as well as the Colt strike. Certainly the efforts of the Jay, Maine, paperworkers stand out: On numerous occasions, they participated in Colt strike support activities and their accounts of their strike support activities often seemed to surpass the efforts of the CLA. Moreover, the successful efforts of the United Mine Workers in their Pittston strike provided dramatic new examples of labor activism, in many ways far surpassing the achievements of Hartford's CLA.

I have emphasized the role of neighborhood organizations in electoral work, specifically their refraining from partisan participation, and traced this to two factors: methodological considerations and funding considerations. Several neighborhood organization staff members vehemently oppose partisan electoral participation, and all of the organizations are expressly prohibited from such participation by their bylaws, so as to conform with funding restrictions. Whether neo-Alinsky organizations in other cities share this orientation or are similarly constrained by funders may affect the direction of local political initiatives and indeed national electoral developments. Moreover, the general disposition toward coalition work may vary greatly among different neo-Alinsky organizations and national networks. Hartford's organizations happen to take the particular stances described earlier, but if other organizations view coalitions differently, the coalition work in their communities may proceed much more easily.

We can generalize that individuals do look for ways to respond to problems and express their frustrations in their workplaces and communities. Whether they find the more constructive outlets of the unions and neighborhood organizations that are available to the respective constituencies in Hartford depends a great deal on labor and community leadership in their particular area. With all of their limitations and despite all of the setbacks and defeats, Hartford's neighborhood groups and labor unions provide the city with leadership who are willing to innovate, take risks, and aggressively work to move their members and participants toward the elusive goal of empowerment.

Both forms of organizing impact the Hartford community, qualitatively and quantitatively, subjectively for individuals who participate and objectively for the conditions in the larger community. They are not necessarily equivalent, but in combination they offer members and participants a greater opportunity for control over their lives, and that opportunity is all that they can promise.

IMPLICATIONS FOR FURTHER RESEARCH, THEORY, AND PRACTICE

Typically, case studies of economic restructuring focus on industries, regions, or cities, rather than on labor or community organizations and their specific adjustments or adaptations to the socioeconomic environment. However, authors such as Smith and Tardanico (1987) call for an examination of the microstructures of social, economic, and political life as an essential component in adequately theorizing about economic and spatial restructuring. They argue specifically for consideration of the household unit and household activities as "basic elements of group and class formation in any social system" (100). Groups such as neighborhood organizations and local labor unions are also among such microstructures immediately outside the household unit. Moreover, their concern for the adaptive strategies of low-income households is relevant to the neighborhood organizations and labor unions.

> Even when popular movements are weak or non-existent, knowledge about the political significance of the interplay between work and residential arrangements is vital for evaluating the latent political interests and capacities of the urban working classes. Such interests and capacities must be taken into account as we consider the consequences of state and business policies; the options of powerful interests, such as government officials, party organizations, domestic entrepreneurs and foreign investors; and the potential outcomes of social, economic and political crises. . . . In light of the everyday networks of low-income people, their role in urban politics directs attention to this question: To what degree, and how, does the interplay of relations to workplace, household and neighborhood influence their political interests and capacity for political action? (102).

They further specify a research agenda that includes local-level questions and issues.

1. What social networks are created within, between and outside households by the income-producing and culturally reproductive activities of the urban popular classes?
2. What cooperative and conflicting social interests are generated by such networks, and what resources can be mobilized on behalf of the various interests?
3. How do such networks, interests and resources interact with the organization and control of production as well as with the structure and policies of the state to promote or impede work-based and community-based political action? (106).

I have begun to address these questions at a level of social organization outside the household, but still quite within the grasp of the "urban popular classes" to which they refer. The adaptive strategies of the two types of organizations and their implications for local politics in Hartford speak to the concerns of Smith and Tardanico. I have emphasized just how important the strategic choices made by organizational leadership are. Moreover, these choices are not necessarily predictable or predetermined and are not often considered in the discussion of popular responses to restructuring. They warrant closer attention.

Some of these choices involve strategic patterns in which, despite a very inhospitable climate for such demands, labor has attempted to recast issues like major strikes or plant closings as public issues and demands with communitywide and regional implications. Local and state levels of government are called upon to mitigate the effects of problems heretofore considered "private" matters between employer and employees, and not the responsibility of government. In other words, labor is attempting to redefine both public discourse and public action in response to contemporary economic problems. Despite success or failure, the fact that these issues surface in the public arena and that labor sometimes succeeds demonstrates that popular praxis *does* matter and can create new options even in the face of the immense obstacles.

Gottdiener's *The Decline of Urban Politics* (1987) generated discussion over the question of whether a genuine urban politics can or does exist, given both the historical evolution and juridical limitations of authority of the local state, especially in the context of economic and political restructuring and the emerging global urban hierarchy. His work was published well after I began to work on this project. However, since he concludes that the possibilities for urban politics have been greatly diminished, I feel compelled to offer a response based on the Hartford experiences.

First, Clarke and Kirby's (1990) critique of Gottdiener seems a convincing one, summarized particularly well in their invoking the metaphor of Mark Twain's comment upon reading his own obituary that reports of his death were "much exaggerated." Urban politics may be greatly constrained or circumscribed and participation may have greatly contracted, yet it seems hardly accurate to announce its demise. In Hartford, urban politics is very animated: The contests and policy debates translate into discernible issues for the local electorate and citizenry, despite all of the constraints upon local government. Clarke and Kirby comment:

> Deducing local political change from spatial configurations or economic logic leaves huge silences about the people affected by economic transformation and their varying responses to these changes. An alternative interpretation of global economic change (from Gottdiener's) emphasized the destabilizing effects of changing investment and migration patterns for communities and households (Feagin and Smith, 1987a:24). . . . Is this deathly local silence that Gottdiener anticipated in the unfolding logic of capitalist development, or does it signal the lag in political development and institutional change that so often characterizes momentous economic transformation? Obviously, we argue for the latter. . . .
>
> Many of the researchers in this field echo Gottdiener's somber view of the increasing constraints on local politics but are informed by a view of history that is less equifinal and linear than his approach. In consequence, researchers allow for contingent local responses and hold open the possibility that these same structural conditions that Gottdiener interprets as sounding the death knell of local politics also contain the seeds of future political change. Harvey's (1987:280) view of emergent flexible accumulation processes, for example, allowed for contingent local responses and "new paths of social change," including resistance and empowerment of worker and community groups. As he put it, the deconcentration and decentralization accompanying these new processes create a political climate "in which the politics of community, place, and region can unfold in new ways" (p. 279). M. P. Smith (1987:244) also

was optimistic that this era of fiscal austerity, wage cuts, productivity measures, sectoral restructuring, and privatization may, nevertheless, offer grounds for overcoming historical cleavages between community and workplace. (401)

Clarke and Kirby characterize cities as "contested areas shaped by economic agents and political actors" (407). The issues in Hartford that I have analyzed here illustrate the politics of economic restructuring and the forces at a city's grassroots level that influence and shape the outcomes. Local developments in Hartford indeed correspond to the "lag in political development" inherent in popular response to economic transformation. What a municipal government does in the face of economic restructuring, and how communities respond and organize, are by no means predetermined: Choices that people at the grassroots level make in their unions and neighborhoods make a difference.

Several patterns I have identified in Hartford involve attempts by labor and community organization forces to coalesce and to bridge the gap between workplace and community. However, even though an event like the Colt strike wrought financial hardship for those involved, these patterns of coalition building were observed during a period of relative economic growth within the context of restructuring, the mid- to late 1980s. In the early 1990s, the state of Connecticut endured a recession and a state tax and budget crisis, and Hartford confronted a series of local municipal fiscal crises. The patterns of coalescence during the 1980s are altering in the '90s as the very participants in these coalitions compete with each other for scarcer and scarcer resources. Within these developments, choices and assessments by organizational leadership will be of paramount importance to the outcomes.

It seems an open question whether under these conditions the coalitions between labor and community forces will strengthen or deepen, no matter how desirable this might be as a means of increasing the potential of local social change movements. If the coalition efforts can maintain themselves and not diminish, then some lasting results may have been created during the 1980s. But a true assessment needs to include consideration of how lasting the coalition efforts are. I am cautious in the light of the constraints on neighborhood organizations within their methodology and philosophy, and, moreover, because of constraints on the resources of the labor unions involved and the relative importance attached to such endeavors by their leaderships. Perhaps if there were more common organizational processes and targets, or more similarity in the obstacles faced by the organizations, lasting coalitions would be easier to construct. Given these issues, the dichotomy between community and workplace continues, but perhaps the chasm is not as deep as it once was.

It is likely that in many cities local electoral activities will command greater energies, but in a new mode akin to the People for Change effort either within or outside of the Democratic party. I have outlined the reasons why an actual third party may not seem appropriate or possible for other cities, but insurgent electoral formations or groupings are forming and have formed, breathing life into the moribund urban politics Gottdiener decries. One problem inherent in Hartford that could emerge elsewhere is that such efforts depend in large measure upon activist unions. The resources of these unions will probably become more strained in the future unless they can organize large numbers of currently unorganized workers. In a recession, this is exceedingly difficult, and as a result, insurgent electoral efforts that depend upon these unions may suffer, although not falter entirely. In other cities neighborhood and community organizations with more open leadership may play a greater supportive role in such electoral efforts.

The ability of unions to organize in the immediate future can have wide implications. A reinvigorated labor movement, particularly with respect to its organizing capacity, could animate other social movements and transform the specific issues of labor into issues with broader appeal. Organizing drives, as well as strikes or plant closings, can be orchestrated in ways that involve many segments of a community and raise a variety of ancillary issues with civil rights, civil liberties, and other equity implications. If larger sections of the labor movement take their lead from the activities of the unions examined in this research, then such a revitalized labor movement may begin to accomplish the mission it purports to champion, the empowerment of workers. More likely, there will be some segments of the labor movement who will attempt to organize the unorganized, but other segments who will be incapable of rising to the occasion.

Neighborhood movements offer great potential as a way of alleviating urban problems, but here again, the important factors of leadership judgment and capacity to reevaluate models and assumptions will figure prominently into whether or not these organizations live up to their promise. In Hartford, the problems of the city seem to become more and more entrenched and complex, and the neighborhood organizations are faced with confronting these difficulties without necessarily devoting sufficient effort toward analysis and sharpening of method. Perhaps neighborhood organizing in Hartford has reached a plateau that may require reformulation from the national organizing networks, although disseminating any such conclusions or consensus will be difficult, given the resistance of Hartford's local organizations to outside advice.

TO CONCLUDE: DON'T MOURN, ORGANIZE!

The vice-president for organizing in 1199–New England, David Pickus, describes his approach to potential members: He tells them that he is not a salesman, he is not selling encyclopedias, he is offering them a vehicle for them to help themselves, and if they want it, they will have to work to get it. That is perhaps less eloquent than Frederick Douglass's statement that power concedes nothing without a struggle, but an apt assessment of the work of his union and that of the other organizations in Hartford. Certainly they are among the most visible vehicles for social change at the grassroots level or on the shop floor.

These movements and activities need to be examined more

thoroughly and factored into theoretical formulations of economic change. The participants themselves need to scrutinize the methodologies and assumptions of their organizations. There is no easy advice to offer in either endeavor since the unfolding of urban social change rests on so many indeterminate and distinct issues, all overlaid by issues of equity and race relations. I have attempted to explore and analyze what has transpired in Hartford. I hope these experiences provide insights into the important changes underway in American cities.

Progressive forces in the cities and elsewhere must continue organizing for just and humane causes. In the end, only these efforts will soften the blows of the economy and forge needed change.

EPILOGUE

Events and developments that occurred after the period generally covered in this book—particularly after my election to the Hartford City Council on the People for Change slate in 1991—totally overtook my life, my schedule, and my perspectives on issues. Along with the mayor and council colleagues, I became a target of protest and the object of derision by local radio talk shows and the editorial boards of the local press. I was responsible for voting on budgets, collective-bargaining contracts, policy directions and initiatives, and the selection of city administrators. All of this is in the context of one of the most dire and ongoing fiscal crises in Hartford's history and for most major cities generally. The 1992 Los Angeles experience brought an even greater sense of social crisis to all our deliberations.

As our resources have diminished, the possibilities for coalition building have indeed worsened: Some of the very labor and neighborhood organizations I describe argued before the council over city issues. Sadly, political maneuvering splintered and rearranged some of the promising electoral coalitions in the city, resulting in our 1993 loss.

On the council during my first year we had to define success in achieving a balanced budget in terms of city employee wage freezes and increased health insurance copayments in exchange for no layoffs. After spending four years on the Colt picket line fighting union busting, I found myself hoping for concessions by city workers so that their jobs could be saved. In the budget cycle of my second year, Hartford faced a $34 million budget deficit, a bitterly divided council, a crisis in our education budget, municipal unions who wanted no part of any more concessions, and some layoffs ensued. Hard times indeed.

Resource constraints for the city translate into despair in our neighborhoods. Despair translates into violence and self-destructive behavior. Regional disparities between Hartford and its suburbs are not abating, and one economic development alternative that was considered was the building of a gambling casino in downtown Hartford. Hundreds of millions of dollars were spent in aggressive lobbying and public relations campaigns to promote the casino proposal. Many are so desperate for relief that they will grab on to this leaky lifeboat, convinced that building a casino in the nation's eighth-poorest city is a viable solution to poverty. Although the effort in Hartford was quashed in 1993 after political, business, and community opposition, it will surely rise again as a consideration. The debate shifted to locating the casino in Bridgeport, Connecticut, where there is much less opposition. The effort is formidable, with far-reaching tentacles into the political world, preying on desperation.

Certainly there is still life in urban politics, because the needs of cities are so great that they will inevitably animate demands and some type of struggle. The questions remain: What will the nature of the struggle be? How long can we as a society wait to address our urban crisis? How will the people respond to their own state of need? What will our national response be—rebuilding or retreating from responsibility?

America needs to respond to its cities. If our society allows its cities to be destroyed by neglect and division, we will all lose. However one thinks about cities and racial and class divisions—a two-tiered society, a racially and economically polarized society— American urban problems are inextricably linked with national economic problems and national political choices. We have choices as a nation, and we've begun to make new ones. We need to make the right choices—humane choices—for our cities before it is too late.

REFERENCES

Alinsky, Saul D. 1946. *Reveille for Radicals*. Chicago: University of Chicago Press.

———. (1949) 1970. *John L. Lewis: An Unauthorized Biography*. New York: Random House Vintage Edition.

———. 1971. *Rules for Radicals: A Practical Primer for Realistic Radicals*. New York: Random House.

Asylum Hill Organizing Project. 1987. "By-Laws." May.

Bass, Paul. 1990. "No Thanks, Bruce." *Hartford Advocate*. August 6, 4.

Bluestone, Barry, and Bennett Harrison. 1982. *The Deindustrialization of America*. New York: Basic Books.

Brecher, Jeremy, and Tim Costello. 1988a. "American Labor: The Promise of Decline." *Zeta*, May, 75–80.

———. 1988b. "Labor and Community: Converging Programs." *Zeta*, August, 114–20.

———, editors. 1990. *Building Bridges: The Emerging Grassroots Coalition of Labor and Community*. New York: Monthly Review.

Citizen Research Education Network. 1990. "The Hartford Partnership: A Report to the Community." April.

"A City Built on Risk." 1986. Connecticut Old State House Exhibition Brochure. Hartford, Connecticut. May 16–September 14.

Clark, Gordon. 1989. *Unions and Communities Under Seige*. New York: Cambridge University Press.

Clarke, Susan E., and Andrew Kirby. 1990. "In Search of the Corpse: The Mysterious Case of Local Politics." *Urban Affairs Quarterly* 25, no. 3:389–412.

Clavel, Pierre. 1986. *The Progressive City*. New Brunswick, N.J.: Rutgers University Press.

Cloward, Richard, and Frances Fox Piven. 1984. "Introduction." In *Roots to Power: A Manual for Grassroots Organizing,* by Lee Staples. New York: Praeger.

Connecticut Department of Labor, Employment Security Division. 1966. "Total Nonagricultural Employment by Town, Hartford Area, June 1965." Mimeo.

————. 1971. "Total Nonagricultural Employment by Town, Hartford Area, June 1970." Mimeo.

————. 1976. "Total Nonagricultural Employment by Town, Hartford Area, June 1975." Mimeo.

————. 1981. "Total Nonagricultural Employment by Town, Hartford Area, June 1980." Mimeo.

————. 1982. "Total Nonagricultural Employment by Town, Hartford Area, June 1981." Mimeo.

————. 1983. "Total Nonagricultural Employment by Town, Hartford Area, June 1982." Mimeo.

————. 1984. "Total Nonagricultural Employment by Town, Hartford Area, June 1983." Mimeo.

————. 1985. "Total Nonagricultural Employment by Town, Hartford Area, June 1984." Mimeo.

————. 1986. "Total Nonagricultural Employment by Town, Hartford Area, June 1985." Mimeo.

————. 1987. "Total Nonagricultural Employment by Town, Hartford Area, June 1986." Mimeo.

————. 1988. "Total Nonagricultural Employment by Town, Hartford Area, June 1987." Mimeo.

————. 1989. "Total Nonagricultural Employment by Town, Hartford Area, June 1988." Mimeo.

————. 1990a. "1990 Connecticut Labor Force Data by Place of Residence, Hartford LMA. Revised 3-90." Mimeo.

————. 1990b. "Total Nonagricultural Employment by Town, Hartford Area, June 1989." Mimeo.

————. 1991a. "1989 Connecticut Labor Force Data by Place of Residence, Hartford LMA, Revised 3-91." Mimeo.

————. 1991b. "1988 Connecticut Labor Force Data by Place of Residence, Hartford LMA, Revised 3-91," Mimeo.

————. 1991c. "Total Nonagricultural Employment by Town, Hartford Area, June 1990." Mimeo.

Delgado, Gary. 1986. *Organizing the Movement*. Philadelphia: Temple University Press.

Fainstein, Susan, and Norman Fainstein. 1985. "Economic Restructuring and the Rise of Urban Social Movements." *Urban Affairs Quarterly* 21, no. 2:187–206.

Feagin, Joe R., and Michael Peter Smith. 1987. "Cities and the New International Division of Labor: An Overview." In *The Capitalist City,* edited by Feagin and Smith. Oxford: Basil Blackwell.

Fink, Leon, and Brian Greenberg. 1989. *Upheaval in the Quiet Zone: A*

History of Hospital Workers' Union, Local 1199. Urbana: University of Illinois Press.

Fisher, Robert. 1984. *Let the People Decide: Neighborhood Organizing in America*. Boston: Twayne Publishers.

Goldfield, Michael. 1987. *The Decline of Organized Labor in the United States*. Chicago: University of Chicago Press.

Gottdiener, Mark. 1987. *The Decline of Urban Politics*. Newbury Park, Calif.: Sage.

Harrison, Bennett, and Barry Bluestone. 1988. *The Great U-Turn*. New York: Basic Books.

Hartford Commission on the City Plan. 1984. "Economic and Employment Component: Comprehensive Plan of Development."

Hartford Planning Department. 1983. "Hartford State of the City September 1983."

————. 1986. "Downtown Development Analysis." Mimeo.

————. 1991. "1990 Census Data Release." Mimeo.

Harvey, David. 1987. "Flexible Accumulation Through Urbanization." *Antipode* 19, no. 3:260–86.

Horgan, Sean. 1988. "When Construction Dust Settles, Will the Offices Be Empty?" *Hartford Courant*, June 12, A1, A4.

Johnson, Kirk. 1990. "Hartford, Its Boom Over, Sees Downtown Decaying." *New York Times*, August 22, 1.

Kahn, Si. 1982. *Organizing: A Guide for Grassroots Leaders*. New York: McGraw Hill.

Katznelson, Ira. 1981. *City Trenches*. New York: Pantheon.

Lendler, Marc. 1989. "Ordinary People, Extraordinary Times." Manuscript.

Lipsky, Michael. 1970. *Protest in City Politics*. Chicago: Rand McNally.

Lipton, Eric. 1992. "Hartford Still Among Ten Poorest Cities in Census Report." *Hartford Courant*, December 16, C1, C11.

McCarthy, Peggy. 1988. "In Hartford, the Best and Worst of Times." *New York Times*, February 7, sect. 11, pp. 1, 14.

McKnight, John, and John Kretzman. 1984. "Community Organizing in the 80s: Toward a Post-Alinsky Agenda." *Social Policy* 14 (Winter): 15–17.

Montgomery, David. 1979. *Workers' Control in America*. New York: Cambridge University Press.

"More Job Loss at Travelers." 1989. *Hartford Advocate*, January 30.

Neubeck, Kenneth, and Richard Ratcliff. 1988. "Urban Democracy and the Power of Corporate Capital: Struggles over Downtown Growth and Neighborhood Stagnation in Hartford, Connecticut." In *Business Elites and Urban Development,* edited by Scott Cummings. Albany: SUNY Press.

Pazniokas, Mark. 1988. "Downtown's Daring Rise." *Hartford Courant,* June 12, A1, A10.

Piven, Frances Fox, and Richard Cloward. 1977. *Poor People's Movements.* New York: Vintage Books.

Reitzes, Donald, and Dietrich Reitzes. 1987. *The Alinsky Legacy: Alive and Kicking.* Greenwich, Conn.: JAI Press.

Remez, Michael. 1990. "AFL-CIO Leader Discusses Issues Facing Labor, State." *Hartford Courant Business Weekly,* November 5, 7.

Romash, Marla. 1987. "Community Organizers Are a Changing Breed." *Hartford Courant,* July 24, 1.

Schwartz, Arthur, and Michele Hoyman. 1984. "The Changing of the Guard: The New American Labor Leader." *Annals of the American Academy of Political and Social Science* 473:64–75.

Shapiro, Bruce. 1986. "Democratic Gadfly in Connecticut." *The Nation,* August 30, 140–44.

Simmons, Louise. 1990. "Organizational and Leadership Models in Community-Labor Coalitions." In *Building Bridges: The Emerging Grassroots Coalition of Labor and Community,* edited by Jeremy Brecher and Tim Costello. New York: Monthly Review.

Smith, Michael Peter. 1987. "Global Restructuring and Local Political Crises in U.S. Cities." In *Global Restructuring and Territorial Development,* edited by Jeffrey Henderson and Manuel Castells. London: Sage.

Smith, Michael Peter, and Richard Tardanico. 1987. "Urban Theory Reconsidered: Production, Reproduction, and Collective Action." In *The Capitalist City,* edited by Joe R. Feagin and Michael Peter Smith. Oxford: Basil Blackwell.

Tomlins, Christopher. 1985. *The State and the Unions.* New York: Cambridge University Press.

Williams, Larry. 1988. "A Society Far Apart." *Hartford Courant,* September 25, A1, A15.

INDEX

ACORN. *See* Association of Community Organizations for Reform Now
Aetna Life and Casualty, 8, 88, 129
AFL-CIO, 24, 38–39; and Colt strike, 89; Committee on Political Education (COPE), 102; and LEAP, 63. *See also* Greater Hartford Labor Council
African American community in Hartford, 13
AFSCME. *See* American Federation of State, County and Municipal Employees
AHOP. *See* Asylum Hill Organizing Project
Alinsky, Saul, 18, 22, 147, 149. *See also* Neo-Alinskyism
Allison, Mike, 137
American Federation of Labor and Congress of Industrial Organizations. *See* AFL-CIO
American Federation of State, County and Municipal Employees (AFSCME), 24, 101
Arnold, Rudolph, 14
Association of Community Organizations for Reform Now (ACORN), 22, 165
Asylum Hill, Inc., 139, 140
Asylum Hill Organizing Project (AHOP), 10, 21–22, 109, 112, 117, 120, 136, 142, 150; annual congress, 134; bylaws, 124–25; employment assistance, 139, 140; Housing Coalition, 118–19; newsletter, 129; organizational structure of, 133, 137, 138
Autorino, Anthony, 93

Barrett, E. T. "Ted," 97
Blitz organizing model, 69–72
Bonelli, John, 15
Borges, Francisco, 14
Brecher, Jeremy, 164–65
Brinksmanship, 94–95
Broad-Park Development Corporation, 125, 141
Brown, Jerome (Jerry), 56, 101, 104, 105
Building Trade Unions, 64

Carbone, Nicholas, 13, 14
Caro, Eugenio, 15, 16
Carter, Jimmy, 12
CCAG. *See* Connecticut Citizens Action Group
Citizen Action, 22, 23
Citizen Research Education Network, 131
CLA. *See* Community-Labor Alliance
Clarke, Susan E., 169, 170–71
Clavel, Pierre, 13
Clinton, Bill, 12
Cloward, Richard, 32, 74
Coalitions in Hartford, 31–34, 35–38, 64–66, 162–64; anticrime, 36; electoral, 31, 164–65; experiences within, 44–56; future of, 171–72; importance of, 157–59; outcomes of, 56–63; rationales for involvement in, 38–43. *See also* Community-Labor Alliance; Legislative Electoral Action Program (LEAP); Linkage Coalition; People for Change